WHAT IS ART?

The Library of Liberal Arts
OSKAR PIEST, FOUNDER

WHAT IS ART?

LEO N. TOLSTOY

Translated from the Russian original by
ALMYER MAUDE

With an introduction by
VINCENT TOMAS

. . . .

The Library of Liberal Arts
published by

Macmillan Publishing Company
New York
Collier Macmillan Publishers
London

Leo N. Tolstoy: 1828 - 1910

W HAT IS ART? was originally published in 1896

. . . .

Macmillan Publishing Company
866 Third Avenue
New York, New York, 10022
Collier Macmillan Canada, Inc.

First Edition
PRINTING   21   YEAR   5

Library of Congress Catolog Card Number: 60-9557
ISBN: 0-02-377400-2

CONTENTS

· · · · · · · · · · · · · · · ·

WHAT IS ART?

LEO N. TOLSTOY: A CHRONOLOGY

1828   September 9, birth of Leo Nikolaevich Tolstoy at Yasnaya Polyana, his parents' country estate in the province of Tula.

1831   Death of Tolstoy's mother.

1837   Death of Tolstoy's father. Child subsequently reared by elderly female relatives and educated by French tutors.

1844-1847 Matriculated at Kazan university; left without degree.

1848-1850 Unsuccessful attempt at farming followed by active social life in Moscow and Petersburg.

1851-1857 Career in army; service in the Caucasus and Crimean War; commanded battery at Sevastopol, 1855.

1852   Completed and published first story, "Childhood."

1854   Completed story "The Cossacks."

1857   Baudelaire's *Les Fleurs du Mal* is published. Travel in Europe.

1861   Return to Yasnaya Polyana; started school for peasant children; emancipated his serfs in accordance with provisions of the Emancipation Act; published a journal devoted to the advancement of his pedagogical ideas.

1862   Marriage to Sophie Behrs, 16 years his junior.

1866   Completed *War and Peace.*

1876   Turning point of his religious life.

1877   Completed *Anna Karenina* which he had begun four years earlier.

1884   Completed *The Death of Ivan Ilyich.*

1889   *Power of Darkness,* the first of several plays.

1896   Publication of *What Is Art?*

1901   Excommunication by the Synod of the Russian Church.

1910   November 8, death in station-master's room at Astapovo (gov. of Ryazan). Interred at Yasnaya Polyana without a Christian burial.

INTRODUCTION

THE first uncensored edition of Leo Tolstoy's *What Is Art?* appeared in an English translation in 1898. Today, more than sixty years later, the book remains one of the most vigorous attacks upon formalism and the doctrine of art for art's sake ever written. When Tolstoy wrote, the process that José Ortega y Gasset was later to describe as "the dehumanization of art" was only in its beginning. But with unerring instinct Tolstoy perceived the tendencies toward depreciation of subject matter, toward unintelligibility and exclusiveness, and toward the "divorce of art from life" that were to become more and more dominant features of "modern art" in the twentieth century. Since Tolstoy decried these tendencies, it would be easy for many of his present-day readers for whom they represent what is fresh, experimental, and creative in contemporary art to judge Tolstoy's views on the nature, function, and value of art to be merely simple-minded and reactionary. To do so, however, would be a mistake. While there is no denying that Tolstoy's theory is one-sided and, in some respects, even fanatical, it is, when seen in broad outline, a coherent and plausible alternative to other equally one-sided and fanatical views, which are fashionable today, and for which it may suggest needed qualifications and corrections. And this is in addition to its historical importance. It seemed to Roger Fry that the appearance in Tolstoy's book of the idea that art is the transmission of an emotion felt by the artist marks "the beginning of fruitful speculation in aesthetics." [1]

Tolstoy begins his reflections by adopting the perspective of a man from Mars who, though he is endowed with intelligence and good will toward the human race, knows nothing about the inner meaning of the activities they call "art" engaged in by the human beings he is observing. He notes that they de-

[1] *Vision and Design.* New York, 1932, p. 293.

vote an enormous amount of time, labor, and money to the creation, exhibition, performance, appreciation, and criticism of paintings, statues, dramas, operas, dances, music, and poetry. He observes that:

> Not only is enormous labor spent on this activity, but in it, as in war, the very lives of men are sacrificed. Hundreds of thousands of people devote their lives from childhood to learning to twirl their legs rapidly (dancers), or to touch notes and strings very rapidly (musicians), or to sketch with paint and represent what they see (artists), or to turn every phrase inside out and find a rhyme to every word. And these people, often very kind and clever and capable of all sorts of useful labor, grow savage over their specialized and stupefying occupations, and become one-sided and self-complacent specialists, dull to all the serious phenomena of life and skilful only at rapidly twisting their legs, their tongues, or their fingers (p. 10).[2]

From the same deliberately naïve point of view, Tolstoy describes a rehearsal of an opera and, in an appendix, the contents of Richard Wagner's *Nibelungen Ring*.

Of course what results, from the point of view of those being observed, is caricature; and some of Tolstoy's critics have succumbed to the temptation to dismiss his strictures against much of what passed as "art" in his day, and by extension passes as such in our own, as no more than the petulant expressions of the prejudices of a philistine or a puritan. But one function of caricature is to reveal, through exaggeration, a truth. Tolstoy is undeniably right when he observes that for the sake of something called "art" great "sacrifices of labor, of human life, and even of goodness" must be made. He then asks, perfectly reasonably, "is it true that art is so important that such sacrifices should be made for its sake?" (p. 14).

Some adherents of "art for art's sake" seem to regard it as self-evident that art is self-justifying. All of them answer Tolstoy's question in the affirmative. Tolstoy's own answer is a conditional one. How important art is and what sacrifices it is worth, he believes, will depend upon what is meant by the equivocal word "art." According to him, in some senses of the word art is *not* worth the sacrifices made for it. But in a certain sense of the word—the one Tolstoy first puts forward in Chapter V—"the activity of art is a most important one, as important as the activity of speech itself and as generally diffused" (p. 52).

In chapters II-IV, Tolstoy criticizes the view that art is an activity that is productive of beauty. His principal contentions are as follows.

It would be pointless to attempt to clarify the concept of art by analyzing it in terms of beauty unless we were clear about the nature of beauty. Tolstoy makes an exhaustive review of the diverse definitions of beauty, and he concludes that in the end they all amount to "one and the same thing—namely, the reception by us of a certain kind of pleasure; i.e., we call 'beauty' that which pleases us without evoking in us desire" (p. 43). Beauty, then, is "subjective." By this Tolstoy means that beauty is a relational characteristic of things, like being a certain distance away. Just as Boston is 45 miles away from (relative to) Providence, but not from (relative to) New York, so a thing may be beautiful relative to Jones but not relative to Smith. It follows that although Jones and Smith may both agree that "art is an activity that is productive of beauty," they might completely disagree whether a given activity (e.g., what Michelangelo was doing when he painted the Sistine Chapel or what Kandinsky was doing when he painted his nonrepresentational compositions) produced works that are beautiful and is therefore to be regarded as art.

Why should this result be embarrassing for any aesthetic theory that defines art in terms of beauty? Tolstoy assumes that what the aesthetician who insists on a necessary connection between art and beauty seeks is "a general definition which should apply to all artistic productions, and by reference to which we might decide whether a certain article belonged to the realm of art or not" (p. 43). The aesthetician begins his search for such a definition by labelling "works of art" certain works that he finds beautiful, i.e., which are aesthetically pleasing to him and to those who share his taste. He then looks for the characteristics (such as symmetry, order, proportion, harmony of parts, unity in variety, etc.) common to these works and by virtue of which they are pleasing to him. He finds that these characteristics are, let us say, P, Q, and R. He then concludes that a work of art is whatever has P, Q, and R, and that the activity of art is one that produces such works. Another aesthetician, with a different taste, will begin with a different sample of beautiful works, and he will emerge with a different set of characteristics, say X, Y, and Z, which he will maintain it is necessary for a work to have if it is to be a work of art. Hence no general definition of art satisfactory to everyone can be found by this method, for—

> the theory of art founded on beauty, expounded by aesthetics, and in dim outline professed by the public, is nothing but the setting up as good of that which has pleased and pleases us, i.e., pleases a certain class of people (p. 45).

Another of Tolstoy's assumptions is that taste, which we may here understand to mean the capacity of an individual to be aesthetically pleased by certain works and displeased by certain others, is not the final arbiter of what is good and bad art, and it is not by reference to taste that we can settle the question whether the production, display, and appreciation of art are important or trivial activities, and worth the sacrifices they entail. To deny this assumption, he contends, would be like maintaining that the importance of producing, preparing, and eating food is to be judged merely in terms of the pleasure or displeasure we get from eating, and that the best food is that which has the most pleasant taste. Just as some food that an individual finds pleasant to eat may be correctly judged quite harmful when regarded in its connection with his health and longevity, so something that is aesthetically pleasing may, when seen "in its connection with other phenomena of life" (p. 46), be judged harmful and bad.

Tolstoy then asks, at the beginning of Chapter V, "What is

art—if we put aside the conception of beauty, which confuses the whole matter?" Like many other writers, Tolstoy is not clearly aware of the manifold ambiguities that lurk in the seemingly straightforward question, "What is art?" What is it, exactly, that a person wants to find out if he asks this question? Does he want to find out how the word "art" is commonly used? Does he want to find out how it may best be defined for some theoretical purpose? Or does he perhaps not want to find out anything at all, but rather to issue a manifesto intended to influence the practice of artists and critics? All three of these motives may be detected at work in Tolstoy's book, but what he mainly wanted to know when he asked his question, at least so it seems from the answer that he proposes for it, was, "What noble purpose are painting, sculpture, music, literature, and the other arts fit to serve in the life of man?" Like R. G. Collingwood, who came after him, Tolstoy does not deny that the various activities *called* "art" serve many different purposes. But what purpose, of these, are they *especially* suited for, such that the importance and dignity we attach to them is justifiable? And he holds that this purpose is not to give enjoyment, not to entertain, not to depict reality, though the arts can do these things, but to transmit feelings:

> *To evoke in oneself a feeling one has experienced, and having evoked it in oneself, then, by means of movements, lines, colors, sounds, or forms expressed in words, so to transmit that feeling that others experience the same feeling— this is the activity of art.*
>
> *Art is a human activity consisting in this, that one man consciously, by means of external signs, hands on to others feelings he has lived through, so that other people are infected by these feelings and also experience them* (p. 51).

Art, so conceived, is the language of feelings, coordinate with speech, which is the language of thought. The noble function it is uniquely fitted to perform is that of educating the feelings of men. Through speech, the thoughts of others, contemporaries or those long dead, are made accessible to a man; through art, all that is being lived through by his contemporaries is accessible to him, as well as the feelings experienced by men thousands of years ago, and he has also the possibility of transmitting his own feelings to others.

If people lacked the capacity to receive the thoughts conceived by the men who preceded them and to pass on to others their own thoughts, men would be like wild beasts. . . .

And if men lacked this other capacity of being infected by art, people might be almost more savage still, and, above all, more separated from, and more hostile to, one another.

And therefore the activity of art is a most important one, as important as the activity of speech itself and as generally diffused (p. 52).

Tolstoy's conception of art has roots that can be traced back through Eugene Véron, whose *L'Esthétique* (1878) he had read, and Romanticism at least to Aristotle. It does not supersede, but rather it generalizes Aristotle's theory of tragedy, according to which tragedy "infects," to use Tolstoy's term, the spectator with pity and fear. Not only pity and fear, but any nuance of feeling can be the subject matter of art.[3]

He differs from those Romanticists who regarded art as "the spontaneous overflow of powerful feeling" not only in that he denies that the feeling need be "powerful," but also in that he denies that art is a "spontaneous overflow" of feeling. A spontaneous overflow would be a yawn of boredom or swearing when one hits one's thumb with a hammer. And where Thomas de Quincey distinguished between the literature of knowledge and the literature of power ("the function of the first is *to teach,* of the second *to move;* the first is a rudder, the second is an oar or a sail") Tolstoy, using a strikingly similar metaphor, distinguishes the function of science, which employs speech, from that of art:

Science and art are like a certain kind of barge with kedge-anchors which used to ply on our rivers. Science, like the boats which took the anchors up-stream and made them secure, gives direction to the forward movement, while art,

[3] Cf. p. 51.

like the windlass worked on the barge to draw it toward the anchor, causes the actual progression (p. 181).

Corresponding to De Quincey's distinction is Véron's distinction between the language of "prose" and that of "poetry," the latter being "the external manifestation, by means of lines, colors, movements, sounds, or words, of emotions felt by man." Tolstoy, who owes more to Véron than he ever acknowledges, disagrees with Véron's conception of language on two points. Whereas Véron, like the Romanticists, did not insist that in art the external manifestation of feelings must be *intentional,* Tolstoy does. Also unlike Véron, he holds that by definition language is not merely the external manifestation (expression) of an internal psychical state, but the *communication* of it from one mind to another. Véron's definition, he writes, "is inexact because a man may express his emotions by means of lines, colors, sounds, or words, and yet not act on others by such expression—and then the manifestation of his emotions is not art" (p. 48).

Central to Tolstoy's view are the notions of "infection" and "sincerity." A work of art infects a spectator of it with a feeling in the sense that it causes the spectator actually to undergo —to live through—that feeling. There is no infection if the spectator is caused merely to think of or to imagine the feeling. If one is witnessing a performance of *Othello,* and understands that Othello is jealous, but is not himself also jealous, he has not been infected. Or, if one is listening to music of the sort that one spontaneously describes as joyous, but is not oneself made joyous by what one hears, one has not been infected by the music. Tolstoy recounts:

> A few days ago I was returning home from a walk feeling depressed, as occurs sometimes. On nearing the house I heard the loud singing of a large choir of peasant women. They were welcoming my daughter, celebrating her return home after her marriage. In this singing, with its cries and clanging of scythes, such a definite feeling of joy, cheerfulness, and energy was expressed that, without noticing how it infected me, I continued my way toward the house in a

better mood and reached home smiling and quite in good spirits (p. 134).

Tolstoy never considers the fact that there is a sense in which a piece of music such as that sung by the peasant women may be said to express or to objectify joy, so that an auditor is aware of it *as* "joyous," not "sad," even if at the time he himself is depressed and continues to be so after the music is finished. Later writers, such as Carroll C. Pratt and Suzanne K. Langer, although they agree with Tolstoy that music is a language of emotions, make this sense of expression, rather than Tolstoy's notion of infection, fundamental in their theories of art. But for Tolstoy, music cannot "express" joy to a listener except in the sense that it has the capacity to cause joy in him.

Furthermore, according to Tolstoy, if art is to occur, not only must the work evoke an actual feeling in the spectator, but the artist himself must also have been infected with the same feeling, and then have fashioned the work with the intention that it should be what T. S. Eliot was later to call an "objective correlative." The objective correlative is in effect a substitute stimulus for a feeling aroused in the artist by some stimulus other than a work of art—by some real or imagined "life situation," such as bereavement. The picture that is conjured up is that of a composer or poet who is grieved by the loss of a loved one, who then deliberately writes music or poetry which, when heard by others, will make them feel grief just as he himself felt it.

If the decisions an artist makes when creating his work are not dictated by his impulse to objectify precisely a feeling he has himself lived through, if for example they are instead dictated by his belief that doing so-and-so rather than such-and-such will make the work such that it will arouse in the spectators a feeling not the artist's own (as when a cynical demagogue evokes in his audience patriotic sentiments he does not feel), the artist is "insincere." Tolstoy writes that "the artist should be impelled by an inner need to express his feeling. . . . if the artist is sincere he will express the feeling as he experienced it" (p. 141). If he does otherwise, what results will not be a work of art but a work of "counterfeit art."

Tolstoy contends that the degree of infectiousness of a work of art depends upon "the greater or lesser force with which the artist himself feels the emotions he transmits" (p. 140), since as soon as the spectator realizes that the artist "does not himself feel what he wishes to express—but is doing it for him, the receiver, a resistance immediately springs up, and the most individual and the newest feelings and the cleverest technique not only fail to produce any infection but actually repel" (p. 141). It would seem from this that if an actor is playing Othello in a jealous rage when he himself is not in a jealous rage, the actor is not "sincere." Evidently few if any actors who have played Othello can have been genuine artists, on Tolstoy's view.

George Bernard Shaw wrote that Tolstoy's conception of art as the intentional transmission of feelings is "the simple truth: the moment it is uttered, whoever is really conversant with art recognizes in it the voice of the master." But Shaw's friend and biographer, St. John Ervine, makes the following observation in his *Bernard Shaw: His Life, Work and Friends:*

> Had G. B. S. been more familiar with the stage and less addicted to the society of "intellectual" actresses, he would have known that players commonly carry on private conversations during a play. It is recorded that Irving, while playing Othello and engaged in throttling Desdemona, asked the actress who took her part what they were having for supper that night, for he lodged with her mother, and as she breathed her last groan, she told him (pp. 294-295).

In his theory of criticism, Tolstoy holds that a work of art is subject to evaluation with respect to its form and with respect to its subject matter. He does not analyze these difficult notions but assumes, without question or trepidation, that in every work of art we can distinguish *what* is transmitted (subject matter) from *how* this is done (form). The subject matter of a work is the feeling it transmits. Thus, he claims, the subject matter of the upper class art of his day is limited to "the feeling of pride, the feeling of sexual desire, and the feeling of weariness of life" (p. 74).

If we ignore subject matter and evaluate only the form of a work of art, its quality is directly proportional to its infectiousness: *"The stronger the infection the better is the art"* (p. 140), that is, the better is the form. This criterion for the formal value of a work of art is extremely obscure indeed, and it is not made less so by Tolstoy's account of the three conditions, the most important of which is sincerity, upon which it depends. How, in practice, do we recognize the degree of infectiousness of a work of art? Sometimes Tolstoy holds that if our taste has not been perverted by counterfeit art, we just do. "For a country peasant of unperverted taste this is as easy as it is for an animal of unspoiled scent to follow the trace he needs among a thousand others in wood or forest" (p. 133). But sometimes it seems as if for Tolstoy "infectiousness" is just his way of speaking about the aesthetic effect of a work of art, an effect which is slight or profound depending upon the "rightness" or "fittingness" of its formal elements and which we recognize by aesthetic intuition. At any rate, so it seems to the present writer when Tolstoy writes:

> It is the same in all arts: a wee bit lighter, a wee bit darker, a wee bit higher, lower, to the right or the left—in painting; a wee bit weaker or stronger in intonation, a wee bit sooner or later—in dramatic art; a wee bit omitted, over-emphasized, or exaggerated—in poetry, and there is no contagion. Infection is only obtained when an artist finds those infinitely minute degrees of which a work of art consists, and only to the extent to which he finds them (p. 116f.).

If for the words "contagion" and "infection" in this passage one were to substitute "significant form," Clive Bell would have found nothing to object to in it.

The criterion of value for subject matter is: *the better the feeling transmitted, the better the work of art* in respect to its subject matter. And to decide the relative value of feelings, we must refer to "the religious perception of the age." For

Tolstoy, this was embodied in simple Christianity—in "the consciousness that our well-being, both material and spiritual, individual and collective, temporal and eternal, lies in the growth of brotherhood among all men—in their loving harmony with one another" (p. 145). To the degree that a work of art transmits feelings which tend to unite mankind in brotherhood, or simple feelings of common life consistent with this, it is good. And to the degree that it does otherwise, it is bad.

Such, in brief outline, are Tolstoy's theories of art and art criticism. As Tolstoy presents them, they are enmeshed with one another and with a great many critical judgments of works of art. In the latter, Tolstoy very severely downgrades such exalted figures as the Greek tragedians, Michelangelo, Shakespeare, and Beethoven by applying to their works standards derived from what he believed to be man's highest religious perception. It is these passages, which are frequent, that are likely to capture the reader's attention, as they did that of Tolstoy's contemporaries. Correctly to appraise Tolstoy's views, however, one should try to bear in mind while reading him that most of the remarks he makes *qua* critic of art are not logically implied by the remarks he makes *qua* theorist of art and art criticism, and that if one rejects the standards he applies to the subject matter of art, this may well be because one disagrees with Tolstoy's beliefs about the "meaning of life" rather than because one disagrees with him about the nature and function of art.

VINCENT TOMAS

SELECTED BIBLIOGRAPHY[1]

Bell, Clive. *Art*. London, 1914.
Collingwood, R. G. *The Principles of Art*. London, 1938.
Ducasse, C. J. *Art, the Critics, and You*. New York, 1944.
—— *The Philosophy of Art*. New York, 1929.
Hanslick, Eduard. *The Beautiful in Music*. New York, 1957.
Langer, Susanne K. *Feeling and Form*. New York, 1953.
Meyer, Leonard B. *Emotion and Meaning in Music*. Chicago, 1956.
Véron, Eugene. *Aesthetics*. London, 1879.

NOTE ON THE TEXT

The present edition is a reprint of the original American edition published in 1899 by Thomas Y. Crowell & Co., New York.

The edition follows Aylmer Maude's translation with the exception of minor changes. Spelling and punctuation have been modified in accordance with present-day American usage. Notes supplied by the editorial staff of the publisher have been placed in square brackets.

O. P.

[1] This Bibliography lists only important works in the Emotionalist Theory of Art.

WHAT IS ART?

TRANSLATOR'S PREFACE

THE fundamental thought expressed in this book leads inevitably to conclusions so new, so unexpected, and so contrary to what is usually maintained in literary and artistic circles, that although it is clearly and emphatically expressed (and this I hope has not been lost in translation), most readers who wish to possess themselves of it will have to read the work carefully, and to digest it slowly.

Especially the introductory Chapters II, III, IV, and V, need careful perusal by any who, having adopted one or other of the current theories on beauty and art, may find it difficult to abandon a preconceived view and to clear their minds for a fair appreciation of what is new to them.

The first four chapters raise the problem, and tell us briefly what has been said by previous writers. Chapter III gives (in highly condensed form) the substance of the teaching of some sixty philosophers on this subject, and since many of them were extremely confused, the chapter cannot, in the nature of things, be easy reading.

I should like to remark in passing that, though Tolstoy in this chapter (presumably for convenience of verification) refers chiefly to the compilations of Schasler, Kralik, and Knight, he has gone behind these authorities to the primary sources. To give a single instance: in the paragraph on Darwin, the footnote refers us to Knight, but the remark that the origin of the art of music may be traced back to the call of the males to the females in the animal world will be found in Darwin, but will not be found in Knight.

In Chapter V we come to Tolstoy's definition of art, which definition should be kept well in mind while reading the rest of the book.

No doubt most of those to whom it is an end in itself, who live by it, or make it their chief occupation, will read this book (or leave it unread) and go on in their former way, much as Pharaoh, of old, hardened his heart and did not sympathize with what Moses had to say on the labor question. But for those of us who have felt that art is too valuable a matter to be lost out of our lives, and who, in their quest for social justice, have met the reproach that they were sacrificing the pleasures and advantages of art, this book is of inestimable value in that it solves a perplexed question of far-reaching importance to practical life.

To this class of readers neither the masterly elucidation of the former theories contained in the opening chapters, nor the explanation of how it has come about that such great importance is attached to the activity we call art (Chapters VI and VII), nor the explanation and illustrations of the perversion that art has undergone, nor even the elucidation of the terrible evils this perversion is producing (XVII), will equal in significance the remaining chapters of the book. These show us what to look for in art, how to distinguish it from counterfeits (XV, XVI, and XVIII), treat of the true art of the future (XIX), and explain how science and art are linked together in man's life, are directed by his perception of the meaning of life, and inevitably react on all he thinks and feels.

AUTHOR'S PREFACE

THIS book of mine, *What Is Art?* appears now for the first time in its true form. More than one edition has already been issued in Russia, but in each case it has been so mutilated by the Censor that I request all who are interested in my views on art only to judge of them by the work in its present shape. The causes which led to the publication of the book in a mutilated form—with my name attached to it—were the following: In accordance with a decision I arrived at long ago, not to submit my writings to the Censorship (which I consider to be an immoral and irrational institution), but to print them only in the shape in which they were written—I intended not to attempt to print this work in Russia. However, my good acquaintance, Professor Grote, editor of a Moscow psychological magazine, having heard of the contents of my work, asked me to print it in his magazine and promised me that he would get the book through the Censor's office unmutilated if I would but agree to a few very unimportant alterations, merely toning down certain expressions. I was weak enough to agree to this, and it has resulted in a book appearing under my name from which not only have some essential thoughts been excluded, but into which the thoughts of other men—even thoughts utterly opposed to my own convictions—have been introduced.

The thing occurred in this way. First, Grote softened my expressions, and in some cases weakened them. For instance, he replaced the words "always" by "sometimes," "all" by "some," "Church" religion by "Roman Catholic" religion, "Mother of God" by "Madonna," "patriotism" by "pseudo-patriotism," "palaces" by "palatii," [1] etc., and I did not consider it neces-

[1] Tolstoy's remarks on Church religion were reworded so as to seem to relate only to the Western Church, and his disapproval of luxurious life was made to apply, not, say, to Queen Victoria or Nicholas II, but to the Caesars or the Pharaohs.—Tr.

5

sary to protest. But when the book was already in type, the Censor required that whole sentences should be altered, and that, instead of what I said about the evil of landed property, a remark should be substituted on the evils of a landless prole-tariate.[2] I agreed to this also, and to some further alterations. It seemed not worth while to upset the whole affair for the sake of one sentence, and when one alteration had been agreed to it seemed not worth while to protest against a second and a third. So, little by little, expressions crept into the book which altered the sense and attributed things to me that I could not have wished to say. So that by the time the book was printed it had been deprived of some part of its integrity and sincerity. But there was consolation in the thought that the book even in this form, if it contains something that is good, would be of use to Russian readers whom it would otherwise not have reached. Things, however, turned out otherwise. *Nous comptions sans notre hôte.* After the legal term of four days had already elapsed, the book was seized, and, on instructions received from Petersburg, it was handed over to the Spiritual Censor. Then Grote declined all further participation in the affair, and the Spiritual Censor proceeded to do what he would with the book. The Spiritual Censorship is one of the most ignorant, venal, stupid, and despotic institutions in Russia. Books which disagree in any way with the recognized state religion of Russia, if once it gets hold of them, are almost always totally suppressed and burned, which is what happened to all my religious works when attempts were made to print them in Russia. Probably a similar fate would have overtaken this work also, had not the editors of

---

[2] The Russian peasant is usually a member of a village commune, and has therefore a right to a share in the land belonging to the village. Tol-stoy disapproves of the order of society which allows less land for the support of a village full of people than is sometimes owned by a single landed proprietor. The Censor will not allow disapproval of this state of things to be expressed, but is prepared to admit that the laws and customs, say, of England—where a yet more extreme form of landed prop-erty exists, and the men who actually labor on the land usually possess none of it—deserve criticism.—Tr.

the magazine employed all means to save it. The result of their efforts was that the Spiritual Censor, a priest who probably understands art and is interested in art as much as I understand or am interested in church services, but who gets a good salary for destroying whatever is likely to displease his superiors, struck out all that seemed to him to endanger his position, and substituted his thoughts for mine wherever he considered it necessary to do so. For instance, where I speak of Christ going to the Cross for the sake of the truth He professed, the Censor substituted a statement that Christ died for mankind, i.e., he attributed to me an assertion of the dogma of the Redemption, which I consider to be one of the most untrue and harmful of Church dogmas. After correcting the book in this way, the Spiritual Censor allowed it to be printed.

To protest in Russia is impossible—no newspaper would publish such a protest; and to withdraw my book from the magazine and place the editor in an awkward position with the public was also not possible.

So the matter has remained. A book has appeared under my name containing thoughts attributed to me which are not mine.

I was persuaded to give my article to a Russian magazine in order that my thoughts, which may be useful, should become the possession of Russian readers; and the result has been that my name is affixed to a work from which it might be assumed that I quite arbitrarily assert things contrary to the general opinion, without adducing my reasons; that I only consider false patriotism bad, but patriotism in general a very good feeling; that I merely deny the absurdities of the Roman Catholic Church and disbelieve in the Madonna, but that I believe in the Orthodox Eastern faith and in the Mother of God; that I consider all the writings collected in the Bible to be holy books, and see the chief importance of Christ's life in the Redemption of mankind by His death.

I have narrated all this in such detail because it strikingly illustrates the indubitable truth that all compromise with institutions of which your conscience disapproves—compromises which are usually made for the sake of the general good—instead of producing the good you expected, inevitably lead you, not only to acknowledge the institution you disapprove of, but also to participate in the evil that institution produces.

I am glad to be able by this statement at least to do something to correct the error into which I was led by my compromise.

I have also to mention that besides reinstating the parts excluded by the Censor from the Russian editions, other corrections and additions of importance have been made in this edition.

March 29, 1898.

WHAT IS ART?

CHAPTER ONE

TAKE up any one of our ordinary newspapers and you will find a part devoted to the theater and music. In almost every number you will find a description of some art exhibition, or of some particular picture, and you will always find reviews of new works of art that have appeared, of volumes of poems, of short stories, or of novels.

Promptly, and in detail, as soon as it has occurred, an account is published of how such and such an actress or actor played this or that role in such and such a drama, comedy, or opera, and of the merits of the performance, as well as of the contents of the new drama, comedy, or opera, with its defects and merits. With as much care and detail, or even more, we are told how such and such an artist has sung a certain piece, or has played it on the piano or violin, and what were the merits and defects of the piece and of the performance. In every large town there is sure to be at least one, if not more than one, exhibition of new pictures, the merits and defects of which are discussed in the utmost detail by critics and connoisseurs.

New novels and poems, in separate volumes or in the magazines, appear almost every day, and the newspapers consider it their duty to give their readers detailed accounts of these artistic productions.

For the support of art in Russia (where for the education of the people only a hundredth part is spent of what would be required to give every one the opportunity of instruction), the government grants millions of rubles in subsidies to academies, conservatories, and theaters. In France twenty million francs are assigned for art, and similar grants are made in Germany and England.

In every large town enormous buildings are erected for museums, academies, conservatories, dramatic schools, and for performances and concerts. Hundreds of thousands of workmen—carpenters, masons, painters, joiners, paperhangers, tailors, hairdressers, jewelers, molders, typesetters—spend their whole lives in hard labor to satisfy the demands of art, so that hardly any other department of human activity, except the military, consumes so much energy as this.

Not only is enormous labor spent on this activity, but in it, as in war, the very lives of men are sacrificed. Hundreds of thousands of people devote their lives from childhood to learning to twirl their legs rapidly (dancers), or to touch notes and strings very rapidly (musicians), or to draw with paint and represent what they see (artists), or to turn every phrase inside out and find a rhyme to every word. And these people, often very kind and clever, and capable of all sorts of useful labor, grow savage over their specialized and stupefying occupations, and become one-sided and self-complacent specialists, dull to all the serious phenomena of life and skilful only at rapidly twisting their legs, their tongues, or their fingers.

But even this stunting of human life is not the worst. I remember being once at the rehearsal of one of the most ordinary of the new operas which are produced at all the opera houses of Europe and America.

I arrived when the first act had already begun. To reach the auditorium I had to pass through the stage entrance. By dark entrances and passages I was led through the vaults of an enormous building, past immense machines for changing the scenery and for lighting, and there in the gloom and dust I saw workmen busily engaged. One of these men, pale, haggard, in a dirty blouse, with dirty, work-worn hands and cramped fingers, evidently tired and out of humor, went past me, angrily scolding another man. Ascending by a dark stair, I came out on the boards behind the scenes. Amid various poles and rings and scattered scenery, decorations, and curtains, stood and moved dozens, if not hundreds, of painted and dressed-up men, in costumes fitting tight to their thighs and calves, and also women, as usual, as nearly nude as might be. These were all singers, or members of the chorus, or ballet dancers, waiting their turns. My guide led me across the stage and, by means of a bridge of boards across the orchestra (in which perhaps a hundred musicians of all kinds, from kettle-drum to flute and harp, were seated), to the dark pit-stalls.

On an elevation, between two lamps with reflectors, and in an armchair placed before a music stand, sat the director of the musical part, baton in hand, managing the orchestra and singers, and, in general, the production of the whole opera.

The performance had already begun, and on the stage a procession of Indians who had brought home a bride was being presented. Besides men and women in costume, two other men in ordinary clothes bustled and ran about on the stage; one was the director of the dramatic part, and the other, who stepped about in soft shoes and ran from place to place with unusual agility, was the dancing master, whose salary per month exceeded what ten laborers earn in a year.

These three directors arranged the singing, the orchestra, and the procession. The procession, as usual, was enacted by couples, with tinfoil halberds on their shoulders. They all came from one place and walked round and round again, and then stopped. The procession took a long time to arrange: first, the Indians with halberds came on too late; then, too soon; then, at the right time, but crowded together at the exit; then they did not crowd, but arranged themselves badly at the sides of the stage; and each time the whole performance was stopped and started again from the beginning. The procession was introduced by a recitative delivered by a man dressed up like some variety of Turk, who, opening his mouth in a curious way, sang, "Home I bring the bri-i-ide." He sings and waves his arm (which is of course bare) from under his mantle. The procession begins, but here the French horn, in the accompaniment of the recitative, does something wrong; and the director, with a shudder as if some catastrophe had occurred, raps with his stick on the stand. All is stopped, and the director, turning to the orchestra, attacks the French horn, scolding him in the rudest terms, as cabmen abuse each other, for taking the wrong note. And again the whole thing begins again. The Indians with their halberds again come on, treading softly in their extraordinary boots; again the singer sings, "Home I bring the bri-i-ide." But here the pairs get too close together. More raps with the stick, more scolding, and a recommencement. Again, "Home I bring the bri-i-ide," again the same gesticulation with the bare arm from under the mantle, and again the couples, treading softly with halberds on their shoulders, some with sad and serious faces, some talking and smiling, arrange themselves in a circle and begin to sing. All seems to be going well, but again the stick raps, and the director, in a distressed and angry voice, begins to scold the men and women of the chorus. It appears that when singing they had omitted to raise their hands from time to time in sign of animation. "Are you all dead, or what? Cows that you are! Are you corpses, that you can't move?" Again they start "Home I bring the bri-i-ide," and again, with sorrowful faces, the chorus women sing, first one and then another of them raising their hands. But two chorus girls speak to each other—again a more vehement rapping with the stick. "Have you come here to talk? Can't you gossip at home? You there in red breeches, come nearer. Look toward me! Begin!" Again, "Home I bring the bri-i-ide." And so it goes on for one, two, three hours. The whole of such a rehearsal lasts six hours on end. Raps with the stick, repetitions, placings, corrections of the singers, of the orchestra, of the procession, of the dancers—all seasoned with angry scolding. I heard the words "asses," "fools," "idiots," "swine," addressed to the musicians and singers at least forty times in the course of one hour. And the unhappy individual to whom the abuse is addressed—flutist, hornblower, or singer—physically and mentally demoralized, does not reply and does what is demanded of him. Twenty times is repeated the one phrase, "Home I bring the bri-i-ide," and twenty times the striding about in yellow shoes with a halberd over the shoulder. The conductor knows that these people are so demoralized that they are no longer fit for anything but to blow trumpets and walk about with halberds and in yellow shoes, and that they are also accustomed to dainty, easy living, so that they will put up with anything rather than lose their luxurious life. He therefore gives free vent to his churlishness, especially as he has seen the same thing done in Paris and Vienna, and knows that this is the way the best conductors behave, and that it is a musical tradition of great artists to be so carried away by the great business of their art that they cannot pause to consider the feelings of other artists.

It would be difficult to find a more repulsive sight. I have seen one workman abuse another for not supporting the weight piled upon him when goods were being unloaded, or, at haystacking, the village elder scold a peasant for not making the rick right, and the man submitted in silence. And, however unpleasant it was to witness the scene, the unpleasantness was lessened by the consciousness that the business in hand was needful and important, and that the fault for which the head man scolded the laborer was one which might spoil a needful undertaking.

But what was being done here? For what, and for whom? Very likely the conductor was tired out, like the workman I passed in the vaults; it was even evident that he was; but who made him tire himself? And for what was he tiring himself? The opera he was rehearsing was one of the most ordinary of operas for people who are accustomed to them, but also one of the most gigantic absurdities that could possibly be devised. An Indian king wants to marry; they bring him a bride; he disguises himself as a minstrel; the bride falls in love with the minstrel and is in despair, but afterwards discovers that the minstrel is the king, and everyone is highly delighted.

That there never were, or could be, such Indians, and that they were not only unlike Indians, but that what they were doing was unlike anything on earth except other operas, was beyond all manner of doubt; that people do not converse in such a way as recitative, and do not place themselves at fixed distances in a quartet, waving their arms to express their emotions; that nowhere, except in theaters, do people walk about in such a manner, in pairs, with tinfoil halberds and in slippers; that no one ever gets angry in such a way, or is affected in such a way, or laughs in such a way, or cries in such a way; and that no one on earth can be moved by such performances—all this is beyond the possibility of doubt.

Instinctively the question presents itself: For whom is this being done? Whom *can* it please? If there are, occasionally, good melodies in the opera to which it is pleasant to listen, they could have been sung simply, without these stupid costumes and all the processions and recitatives and hand-wavings.

The ballet, in which half-naked women make voluptuous movements, twisting themselves into various sensual wreathings, is simply a lewd performance.

So one is quite at a loss as to whom these things are done for. The man of culture is heartily sick of them, while to a real workingman they are utterly incomprehensible. If anyone can be pleased by these things (which is doubtful), it can only be some young footman or depraved artisan who has contracted the spirit of the upper classes but is not yet satiated with their amusements and wishes to show his breeding.

And all this nasty folly is prepared, not simply, nor with kindly merriment, but with anger and brutal cruelty.

It is said that it is all done for the sake of art, and that art is a very important thing. But is it true that art is so important that such sacrifices should be made for its sake? This question is especially urgent because art, for the sake of which the labor of millions, the lives of men, and, above all, love between man and man, are being sacrificed—this very art is becoming something more and more vague and uncertain to human perception.

Criticism, in which the lovers of art used to find support for their opinions, has latterly become so self-contradictory that, if we exclude from the domain of art all that to which the critics of various schools themselves deny the title, there is scarcely any art left.

The artists of various sects, like the theologians of the various sects, mutually exclude and destroy themselves. Listen to the artists of the schools of our times, and you will find, in all branches, each set of artists disowning others. In poetry the old Romanticists deny the Parnassiens and the Decadents; the Parnassiens disown the Romanticists and the Decadents; the Decadents disown all their predecessors and the Symbolists; the Symbolists disown all their predecessors and *les mages;* and *les mages* disown all, all their predecessors. Among novelists we have naturalists, psychologists, and "nature-ists," all rejecting each other. And it is the same in dramatic art, in painting, and in music. So art, which demands such tremendous labor sacrifices from the people, which stunts human lives and transgresses against human love, is not only *not* a thing clearly and firmly defined, but is understood in such contradictory ways by its own devotees that it is difficult to say what is meant by art, and especially what is good, useful art— art for the sake of which we might condone such sacrifices as are being offered at its shrine.

CHAPTER TWO

FOR the production of every ballet, circus, opera, operetta, exhibition, picture, concert, or printed book, the intense and unwilling labor of thousands of people is needed at what is often harmful and humiliating work. It were well if artists made all they require for themselves, but, as it is, they all need the help of workmen, not only to produce art, but also for their own usually luxurious maintenance. And, one way or other, they get it, either through payments from rich people or through subsidies given by government (in Russia, for instance, in grants of millions of rubles to theaters, conservatories, and academies). This money is collected from the people, some of whom have to sell their only cow to pay the tax and who never get those aesthetic pleasures which art gives.

It was all very well for a Greek or Roman artist, or even for a Russian artist of the first half of our century (when there were still slaves and it was considered right that there should be), with a quiet mind to make people serve him and his art; but in our day, when in all men there is at least some dim perception of the equal rights of all, it is impossible to constrain people to labor unwillingly for art without first deciding the question whether it is true that art is so good and so important an affair as to redeem this evil.

If not, we have the terrible probability to consider that while fearful sacrifices of the labor and lives of men, and of morality itself, are being made to art, that same art may be not only useless but even harmful.

And therefore it is necessary for a society in which works of art arise and are supported, to find out whether all that professes to be art is really art, whether (as is presupposed in our society) all that which is art is good, and whether it is important and worth those sacrifices which it necessitates. It is still more necessary for every conscientious artist to know this, that he may be sure that all he does has a valid meaning; that it is not merely an infatuation of the small circle of people among whom he lives which excites in him the false assurance that he is doing a good work; and that what he takes from others for the support of his often very luxurious life will be compensated for by those productions at which he works. And that is why answers to the above questions are especially important in our time.

What is this art which is considered so important and necessary for humanity that for its sake these sacrifices of labor, of human life, and even of goodness may be made?

"What is art? What a question! Art is architecture, sculpture, painting, music, and poetry in all its forms," usually replies the ordinary man, the art amateur, or even the artist himself, imagining the matter about which he is talking to be perfectly clear and uniformly understood by everybody. But in architecture, one inquires further, are there not simple buildings which are not objects of art, and buildings with artistic pretensions which are unsuccessful and ugly and therefore cannot be considered as works of art? Wherein lies the characteristic sign of a work of art?

It is the same in sculpture, in music, and in poetry. Art, in all its forms, is bounded on one side by the practically useful, and on the other by unsuccessful attempts at art. How is art to be marked off from each of these? The ordinary educated man of our circle, and even the artist who has not occupied himself especially with aesthetics, will not hesitate at this question either. He thinks the solution has been found long ago and is well known to everyone.

"Art is such activity as produces beauty," says such a man.

If art consists in that, then is a ballet or an operetta art? you inquire.

"Yes," says the ordinary man, though with some hesitation, "a good ballet or a graceful operetta is also art in so far as it manifests beauty."

But without even asking the ordinary man what differentiates the "good" ballet and the "graceful" operetta from their opposites (a question he would have much difficulty in answering), if you ask him whether the activity of costumers and hairdressers, who ornament the figures and faces of the women for the ballet and the operetta, is art, or the activity of Worth, the dressmaker, or of scent-makers and men cooks— then he will, in most cases, deny that their activity belongs to the sphere of art. But in this the ordinary man makes a mistake just because he is an ordinary man and not a specialist, and because he has not occupied himself with aesthetic questions. Had he looked into these matters, he would have seen in the great Renan's book, *Marc Aurele,* a dissertation showing that the tailor's work is art, and that those who do not see in the adornment of woman an affair of the highest art are very small-minded and dull. "C'est le grand art," says Renan. Moreover, he would have known that in many aesthetic systems—for instance, in the aesthetics of the learned Professor Kralik, *Weltschönheit, Versuch einer allgemeinen Aesthetik, von Richard Kralik,* and in *Les problèmes de l'esthétique con-*

temporaine by Guyau—the arts of costume, of taste, and of
touch are included.

"Es folgt nun ein Fünfblatt von Künsten, die der sub-
jectiven Sinnlichkeit entkeimen" (There results then a penta-
foliate of arts, growing out of the subjective perceptions), says
Kralik (p. 175). "Sie sind die ästhetische Behandlung der fünf
Sinne." (They are the aesthetic treatment of the five senses.)

These five arts are the following:

Die Kunst des Geschmacksinns—The art of the sense of
taste (p. 175).

Die Kunst des Geruchsinns—The art of the sense of smell
(p. 177).

Die Kunst des Tastsinns—The art of the sense of touch
(p. 180).

Die Kunst des Gehörsinns—The art of the sense of hearing
(p. 182).

Die Kunst des Gesichtsinns—The art of the sense of sight
(p. 184).

Of the first of these—*die Kunst des Geschmacksinns*—he
says:

Man hält zwar gewöhnlich nur zwei oder höchstens drei
Sinne für würdig, den Stoff künstlerischer Behandlung
abzugeben, aber ich glaube nur mit bedingtem Recht. Ich
will kein allzugrosses Gewicht darauf legen, dass der
gemeine Sprachgebrauch manch andere Künste, wie zum
Beispiel die Kochkunst, kennt.[1]

And further:

Und es ist doch gewiss eine ästhetische Leistung, wenn es
der Kochkunst gelingt aus einem tierischen Kadaver einen
Gegenstand des Geschmacks in jedem Sinne zu machen. Der
Grundsatz der Kunst des Geschmacksinns (die weiter ist als

[1] Only two, or at most three, senses are generally held worthy to supply matter for artistic treatment, but I think this opinion is only con-
ditionally correct. I will not lay too much stress on the fact that our
common speech recognizes many other arts, as, for instance, the art of
cookery.—Tr.

die sogenannte Kochkunst) ist also dieser: Es soll alles Geniessbare als Sinnbild einer Idee behandelt werden und in jedesmaligem Einklang zur auszudrückenden Idee.[2]

This author, like Renan, acknowledges a *Kostümkunst (Art of Costume,* p. 200), etc.

Such is also the opinion of the French writer, Guyau, who is highly esteemed by some authors of our day. In his book, *Les problèmes de l'esthétique contemporaine,* he speaks seriously of touch, taste, and smell as giving, or being capable of giving, aesthetic impressions:

> Si la couleur manque au toucher, il nous fournit en revanche une notion que l'oeil seul ne peut nous donner, et qui a une valeur esthétique considérable, celle du *doux,* du *soyeux,* du *poli.* Ce qui caractérise la beauté du velours, c'est sa douceur au toucher non moins que son brillant. Dans l'idée que nous nous faisons de la beauté d'une femme, le velouté de sa peau entre comme élément essentiel.
>
> Chacun de nous probablement avec un peu d'attention se rappellera des jouissances du goût, qui ont été de véritables jouissances esthétiques.[3]

And he recounts how a glass of milk drunk by him in the mountains gave him aesthetic enjoyment.

So it turns out that the conception of art as consisting in making beauty manifest is not at all so simple as it seemed,

---

[2] And yet it is certainly an aesthetic achievement when the art of cooking succeeds in making of an animal's corpse an object in all respects tasteful. The principle of the Art of Taste (which goes beyond the so-called Art of Cookery) is therefore this: All that is edible should be treated as the symbol of some idea and always in harmony with the idea to be expressed.

[3] If the sense of touch lacks color, it gives us, on the other hand, a notion which the eye alone cannot afford, and one of considerable aesthetic value, namely, that of softness, silkiness, polish. The beauty of velvet is characterized not less by its softness to the touch than by its luster. In the idea we form of a woman's beauty, the softness of her skin enters as an essential element.

Each of us, with a little effort, can probably recall pleasures of taste which have been real aesthetic pleasures.

especially now, when in this conception of beauty are included our sensations of touch and taste and smell, as they are by the latest aesthetic writers.

But the ordinary man either does not know or does not wish to know all this, and is firmly convinced that all questions about art may be simply and clearly solved by acknowledging beauty to be the subject matter of art. To him it seems clear and comprehensible that art consists in manifesting beauty, and that a reference to beauty will serve to explain all questions about art.

But what is this beauty which forms the subject matter of art? How is it defined? What is it?

As is always the case, the more cloudy and confused the conception conveyed by a word, with the more aplomb and self-assurance do people use that word, pretending that what is understood by it is so simple and clear that it is not worthwhile even to discuss what it actually means.

This is how matters of orthodox religion are usually dealt with, and this is how people now deal with the conception of beauty. It is taken for granted that what is meant by the word beauty is known and understood by everyone. And yet not only is this not known, but, after whole mountains of books have been written on the subject by the most learned and profound thinkers during one hundred and fifty years (ever since Baumgarten founded aesthetics in the year 1750), the question, What is beauty? remains to this day quite unsolved, and in each new work on aesthetics it is answered in a new way. One of the last books I read on aesthetics is a not ill-written booklet by Julius Mithalter, called *Rätsel des Schönen* ("The Enigma of the Beautiful"). And that title precisely expresses the position of the question, What is beauty? After thousands of learned men have discussed it during one hundred and fifty years, the meaning of the word "beauty" remains an enigma still. The Germans answer the question in their manner, though in a hundred different ways. The physiologist-aestheticians, especially the Englishmen Herbert Spencer, Grant Allen, and his school, answer it, each in his own way; the French eclectics and the followers of Guyau and Taine, also each in his own way; and all these people know all the preceding solutions given by Baumgarten, and Kant, and Schelling, and Schiller, and Fichte, and Winckelmann, and Lessing, and Hegel, and Schopenhauer, and Hartmann, and Schasler, and Cousin, and Lévêque, and others.

What is this strange conception "beauty," which seems so simple to those who talk without thinking, but in defining which all the philosophers of various tendencies and different nationalities can come to no agreement during a century and a half? What is this conception of beauty on which the dominant doctrine of art rests?

In Russian, by the word *krasota* (beauty) we mean only that which pleases the sight. And though latterly people have begun to speak of "an ugly deed," or of "beautiful music," it is not good Russian.

A Russian of the common folk, not knowing foreign languages, will not understand you if you tell him that a man who has given his last coat to another, or done anything similar, has acted "beautifully," that a man who has cheated another has done an "ugly" action, or that a song is "beautiful."

In Russian a deed may be kind and good, or unkind and bad. Music may be pleasant and good, or unpleasant and bad; but there can be no such thing as "beautiful" or "ugly" music.

Beautiful may relate to a man, a horse, a house, a view, or a movement. Of actions, thoughts, character, or music, if they please us, we may say that they are good, or, if they do not please us, that they are not good. But beautiful can be used only concerning that which pleases the sight. So the word and conception "good" includes the conception of "beautiful," but the reverse is not the case; the conception "beauty" does not include the conception "good." If we say "good" of an article which we value for its appearance, we thereby say that the article is beautiful; but if we say it is "beautiful" it does not at all mean that the article is a good one.

Such is the meaning ascribed by the Russian language, and therefore by the sense of the people, to the words and conceptions "good" and "beautiful."

In all the European languages, i.e., the languages of those nations among whom the doctrine has spread that beauty is the essential thing in art, the words "beau," "schön," "beautiful," "bello," etc., while keeping their meaning of beautiful in form, have come to also express "goodness," "kindness," i.e., have come to act as substitutes for the word "good."

So it has become quite natural in those languages to use such expressions as "belle âme," "schöne Gedanken," or "beautiful deed." Those languages no longer have a suitable word wherewith expressly to indicate beauty of form, and have to use a combination of words such as "beau par la forme," "beautiful to look at," etc., to convey that idea.

Observation of the divergent meanings which the words "beauty" and "beautiful" have in Russian on the one hand, and in those European languages now permeated by this aesthetic theory on the other hand, shows us that the word "beauty" has, among the latter, acquired a special meaning— namely, that of "good."

What is remarkable, moreover, is that since we Russians have begun more and more to adopt the European view of art, the same evolution has begun to show itself in our language also, and some people speak and write quite confidently, and without causing surprise, of beautiful music and ugly actions, or even thoughts; whereas forty years ago, when I was young, the expressions "beautiful music" and "ugly actions" were not only unusual, but incomprehensible. Evidently this new meaning given to beauty by European thought begins to be assimilated by Russian society.

And what really is this meaning? What is this "beauty" as it is understood by the European peoples?

In order to answer this question I must here quote at least a small selection of those definitions of beauty most generally adopted in existing aesthetic systems. I especially beg the reader not to be overcome by dullness, but to read these extracts through, or, still better, to read some one of the erudite aesthetic authors. Not to mention the voluminous German aestheticians, a very good book for this purpose would be either the German book by Kralik, the English work by Knight, or the French one by Lévêque. It is necessary to read one of the learned aesthetic writers in order to form at first-hand a conception of the variety in opinion and the frightful obscurity which reigns in this region of speculation, not, in this important matter, trusting to another's report.

This, for instance, is what the German aesthetician Schasler says in the preface to his famous, voluminous, and detailed work on aesthetics:

Hardly in any sphere of philosophic science can we find such divergent methods of investigation and exposition, amounting even to self-contradiction, as in the sphere of aesthetics. On the one hand, we have elegant phraseology without any substance, characterized in great part by most one-sided superficiality; and on the other hand, accompanying undeniable profundity of investigation and richness of subject matter, we get a revolting awkwardness of philosophic terminology, infolding the simplest thoughts in an apparel of abstract science, as though to render them worthy to enter the consecrated palace of the system; and finally, between these two methods of investigation and exposition there is a third, forming, as it were, the transition from one to the other, a method consisting of eclecticism, now flaunting an elegant phraseology, and now a pedantic erudition. . . . A style of exposition that falls into none of these three defects but is truly concrete, and, having important matter, expresses it in clear and popular philosophic language, can nowhere be found less frequently than in the domain of aesthetics.[4]

It is only necessary, for instance, to read Schasler's own book to convince oneself of the justice of this observation of his.

[4] M. Schasler, *Kritische Geschichte der ästhetik*, 1872, I, 13.

On the same subject the French writer Véron, in the preface to his very good work on aesthetics, says:

Il n'y a pas de science qui ait été plus que l'esthétique livrée aux rêveries des métaphysiciens. Depuis Platon jusqu' aux doctrines officielles de nos jours, on a fait de l'art je ne sais quel amalgame de fantaisies quintessenciées, et de mystères transcendantaux qui trouvent leur expression suprême dans la conception absolue du Beau idéal, prototype immuable et divin des choses réelles (L'Esthétique, 1878, p. 5).[5]

If the reader will only be at the pains to peruse the following extracts defining beauty taken from the chief writers on aesthetics, he may convince himself that this censure is thoroughly deserved.

I shall not quote the definitions of beauty attributed to the ancients—Socrates, Plato, Aristotle, etc., down to Plotinus—because, in reality, the ancients had not that conception of beauty separated from goodness which forms the basis and aim of aesthetics in our time. By referring the judgments of the ancients on beauty to our conception of it, as is usually done in aesthetics, we give the words of the ancients a meaning which is not theirs.[6]

[5] There is no science which, more than aesthetics, has been handed over to the reveries of the metaphysicians. From Plato down to the received doctrines of our day, people have made of art a strange amalgam of quintessential fancies and transcendental mysteries which find their supreme expression in the conception of an absolute ideal Beauty, immutable and divine prototype of actual things.

[6] See on this matter Benard's admirable book, L'Esthétique d'Aristote, also Walter's Geschichte der Asthetik im Altertum.

CHAPTER THREE

I BEGIN with the founder of aesthetics, Baumgarten (1714-1762).

According to Baumgarten,[1] the object of logical knowledge is truth, the object of aesthetic (i.e., sensuous) knowledge is beauty. Beauty is the Perfect (the Absolute) recognized through the senses; Truth is the Perfect perceived through reason; Goodness is the Perfect reached by moral will.

Beauty is defined by Baumgarten as a correspondence, i.e., an order of the parts in their mutual relations to each other and in their relation to the whole. The aim of beauty itself is to please and excite a desire, *"Wohlgefallen und Erregung eines Verlangens."* (A position precisely the opposite of Kant's definition of the nature and sign of beauty.)

With reference to the manifestations of beauty, Baumgarten considers that the highest embodiment of beauty is seen by us in nature, and he therefore thinks that the highest aim of art is to copy nature. (This position also is directly contradicted by the conclusions of the latest aestheticians.)

Passing over the unimportant followers of Baumgarten—Maier, Eschenburg, and Eberhard—who only slightly modified the doctrine of their teacher by dividing the pleasant from the beautiful, I will quote the definitions given by writers who came immediately after Baumgarten and defined beauty quite in another way. These writers were Sulzer, Mendelssohn, and Moritz. They, in contradiction to Baumgarten's main position, recognize as the aim of art not beauty, but goodness. Thus Sulzer (1720-1777) says that only that can be considered beautiful which contains goodness. According to his theory, the aim of the whole life of humanity is welfare in social life. This is attained by the education of the moral feelings, to which end art should be subservient. Beauty is that which evokes and educates this feeling.

1 Schasler, p. 301.

Beauty is understood almost in the same way by Mendelssohn (1729-1786). According to him, art is the carrying forward of the beautiful, obscurely recognized by feeling, till it becomes the true and good. The aim of art is moral perfection.[2]

For the aestheticians of this school, the ideal of beauty is a beautiful soul in a beautiful body. So these aestheticians completely wipe out Baumgarten's division of the Perfect (the Absolute) into the three forms of Truth, Goodness, and Beauty; and Beauty is again united with the Good and the True.

But this conception is not only not maintained by the later aestheticians, but the aesthetic doctrine of Winckelmann arises, again in complete opposition. This divides the mission of art from the aim of goodness in the sharpest and most positive manner, makes external beauty the aim of art, and even limits it to visible beauty.

According to the celebrated work of Winckelmann (1717-1767), the law and aim of all art is beauty only, beauty quite separated from and independent of goodness. There are three kinds of beauty: (1) beauty of form, (2) beauty of idea, expressing itself in the position of the figure (in plastic art), (3) beauty of expression, attainable only when the two first conditions are present. This beauty of expression is the highest aim of art, and is attained in antique art; modern art should therefore aim at imitating ancient art.[3]

Art is similarly understood by Lessing, Herder, and afterwards by Goethe and by all the distinguished aestheticians of Germany till Kant, from whose day again a different conception of art begins.

Native aesthetic theories arose during this period in England, France, Italy, and Holland, and they, though not taken from the German, were equally cloudy and contradictory. And all these writers, just like the German aestheticians, founded their theories on a conception of the Beautiful, understanding beauty in the sense of a something existing ab-

2 Schasler, p. 369.   3 Schasler, pp. 388-390.

solutely, and more or less intermingled with Goodness or having one and the same root. In England, almost simultaneously with Baumgarten or even a little earlier, Shaftesbury, Hutcheson, Home, Burke, Hogarth, and others wrote on art.

According to Shaftesbury (1670-1713), "That which is beautiful is harmonious and proportionable, what is harmonious and proportionable is true, and what is at once both beautiful and true is of consequence agreeable and good." [4] Beauty, he taught, is recognized by the mind only. God is fundamental beauty; beauty and goodness proceed from the same fount.

So that, although Shaftesbury regards beauty as being something separate from goodness, they again merge into something inseparable.

According to Hutcheson (1694-1747—*Inquiry into the Original of our Ideas of Beauty and Virtue*), the aim of art is beauty, the essence of which consists in evoking in us the perception of uniformity amid variety. In the recognition of what is art we are guided by "an internal sense." This internal sense may be in contradiction to the ethical one. So, according to Hutcheson, beauty does not always correspond with goodness, but separates from it and is sometimes contrary to it.

According to Home, Lord Kames (1696-1782), beauty is that which is pleasant. Therefore beauty is defined by taste alone. The standard of true taste is that the maximum of richness, fullness, strength, and variety of impressions should be contained in the narrowest limits. That is the ideal of a perfect work of art.

According to Burke (1729-1797—*Philosophical Inquiry into the Origin of our Ideas of the Sublime and Beautiful*), the sublime and beautiful, which are the aim of art, have their origin in the promptings of self-preservation and of society. These feelings, examined in their source, are means for the maintenance of the race through the individual. The first

4 Knight, *Philosophy of the Beautiful*, I, 165 f.
5 Schasler, p. 289. Knight, 168 f.

(self-preservation) is attained by nourishment, defense, and war, the second (society) by intercourse and propagation. Therefore, self-defense (and war which is bound up with it) is the source of the sublime; sociability (and the sex instinct, which is bound up with it) is the source of beauty.[6]

Such were the chief English definitions of art and beauty in the eighteenth century.

During that period in France the writers on art were Père André and Batteux, with Diderot, D'Alembert, and, to some extent, Voltaire, following later.

According to Père André (*Essai sur le Beau,* 1741), there are three kinds of beauty—divine beauty, natural beauty, and artificial beauty.[7]

According to Batteux (1713-1780), art consists in imitating the beauty of nature, its aim being enjoyment.[8] Such is also Diderot's definition of art.

The French writers, like the English, consider that it is taste that decides what is beautiful. And the laws of taste are not only laid down, but it is granted that they cannot be settled. The same view was held by D'Alembert and Voltaire.[9]

According to the Italian aesthetician of that period, Pagano, art consists in uniting the beauties dispersed in nature. The capacity to preceive these beauties is taste, the capacity to bring them into one whole is artistic genius. Beauty commingles with goodness so that beauty is goodness made visible, and goodness is inner beauty.[10]

According to the opinion of other Italians, Muratori (1672-1750—*Riflessioni sopra il buon gusto intorno le science e le arti*) and especially Spaletti (*Saggio sopra la bellezza,* 1765) [11] —art amounts to an egotistical sensation founded (as with Burke) on the desire for self-preservation and society.

6 R. Kralik, *Weltschönheit, Versuch einer allgemeinen Aesthetik,* pp. 304-306.

7 Knight, p. 101.   8 Knight, pp. 102-104.

9 Spaletti, Schasler, p. 328.   10 Schasler, p. 316.

11 R. Kralik, p. 124. [*Reflections on the good taste in science and art* and *Essay on beauty.*—Ed.]

Among Dutch writers, Hemsterhuis (1720-1790), who had an influence on the German aestheticians and on Goethe, is remarkable. According to him, beauty is that which gives most pleasure, and that gives most pleasure which gives us the greatest number of ideas in the shortest time. Enjoyment of the beautiful, because it gives the greatest quantity of perceptions in the shortest time, is the highest notion to which man can attain.[12]

Such were the aesthetic theories outside Germany during the last century. In Germany, after Winckelmann, there again arose a completely new aesthetic theory—that of Kant (1724-1804), which, more than all others, clears up what this conception of beauty, and consequently of art, really amounts to.

The aesthetic teaching of Kant is founded as follows: Man has a knowledge of nature outside him and of himself in nature. In nature, outside himself, he seeks for truth; in himself, he seeks for goodness. The first is an affair of pure reason, the other of practical reason (free will). Besides these two means of perception, there is yet the judging capacity (*Urteilskraft*), which forms judgments without reasonings and produces pleasure without desire (*Urteil ohne Begriff, und Vergnügen ohne Begehren*). This capacity is the basis of aesthetic feeling. Beauty, according to Kant, in its subjective meaning is that which, in general and necessarily, without reasonings and without practical advantage, pleases. In its objective meaning it is the form of a suitable object, in so far as that object is perceived without any conception of its utility.[13]

Beauty is defined in the same way by the followers of Kant, among whom was Schiller (1759-1805). According to Schiller, who wrote much on aesthetics, the aim of art is, as with Kant, beauty, the source of which is pleasure without practical advantage. So that art may be called a game, not in the sense of an unimportant occupation, but in the sense of a manifestation of the beauties of life itself without other aim than that of beauty.[14]

12 Schasler, pp. 331-333.   13 Schasler, pp. 525-528.
14 Schasler, pp. 740-743.

Besides Schiller, the most remarkable of Kant's followers in the sphere of aesthetics was Wilhelm Humboldt, who, though he added nothing to the definition of beauty, explained various forms of it—the drama, music, the comic, etc.[15]

After Kant, besides the second-rate philosophers, the writers on aesthetics were Fichte, Schelling, Hegel, and their followers. Fichte (1762-1814) says that perception of the beautiful proceeds from this: the world—i.e., nature—has two sides: it is the sum of our limitations and it is the sum of our free idealistic activity. In the first aspect the world is limited, in the second aspect it is free. In the first aspect every object is limited, distorted, compressed, confined—and we see deformity; in the second we perceive its inner completeness, vitality, regeneration—and we see beauty. So the deformity or beauty of an object, according to Fichte, depends on the point of view of the observer. Beauty therefore exists, not in the world, but in the beautiful soul (*schöner Geist*). Art is the manifestation of this beautiful soul, and its aim is the education, not only of the mind—that is the business of the *savant*, not only of the heart—that is the affair of the moral preacher, but of the whole man. And so the characteristic of beauty lies not in anything external, but in the presence of a beautiful soul in the artist.[16]

Following Fichte, and in the same direction, Friedrich Schlegel and Adam Müller also defined beauty. According to Schlegel (1772-1829), beauty in art is understood too incompletely, one-sidedly, and disconnectedly. Beauty exists, not only in art, but also in nature and in love; so that the truly beautiful is expressed by the union of art, nature, and love. Therefore, as inseparably one with aesthetic art, Schlegel acknowledges moral and philosophic art.[17]

According to Adam Müller (1779-1829), there are two kinds of beauty: the one, general beauty, which attracts people as the sun attracts the planet—this is found chiefly in antique art; and the other, individual beauty, which results from the

15 Knight, pp. 61-63.   16 Schasler, pp. 769-771.
17 Kralik, p. 148.

observer himself becoming a sun attracting beauty—this is the beauty of modern art. A world in which all contradictions are harmonized is the highest beauty. Every work of art is a reproduction of this universal harmony.[18] The highest art is the art of life.[19]

Next after Fichte and his followers came a contemporary of his, the philosopher Schelling (1775-1854), who has had a great influence on the aesthetic conceptions of our times. According to Schelling's philosophy, art is the production or result of that conception of things by which the subject becomes its own object, or the object its own subject. Beauty is the perception of the infinite in the finite. And the chief characteristic of works of art is unconscious infinity. Art is the uniting of the subjective with the objective, of nature with reason, of the unconscious with the conscious, and therefore art is the highest means of knowledge. Beauty is the contemplation of things in themselves as they exist in the prototype (*in den Urbildern*). It is not the artist who by his knowledge or skill produces the beautiful, but the idea of beauty in him itself produces it.[20]

Of Schelling's followers the most noticeable was Solger (1780-1819—*Vorlesungen über Aesthetik*). According to him, the idea of beauty is the fundamental idea of everything. In the world we see only distortions of the fundamental idea, but art, by imagination, may lift itself to the height of this idea. Art is therefore akin to creation.[21]

According to another follower of Schelling, Krause (1781-1832), true, positive beauty is the manifestation of the Idea in an individual form; art is the actualization of the beauty existing in the sphere of man's free spirit. The highest stage of art is the art of life, which directs its activity toward the adornment of life so that it may be a beautiful abode for a beautiful man.[22]

After Schelling and his followers came the new aesthetic

[18] Schasler, pp. 786 f.   [19] Kralik, p. 820.
[20] Schasler, pp. 828 f., 834-841.   [21] Schasler, p. 891.
[22] Schasler, p. 917.

doctrine of Hegel, which is held to this day, consciously by many, but by the majority unconsciously. This teaching is not only no clearer or better defined than the preceding ones, but is, if possible, even more cloudy and mystical.

According to Hegel (1770-1831), God manifests himself in nature and in art in the form of beauty. God expresses himself in two ways: in the object and in the subject, in nature and in spirit. Beauty is the shining of the Idea through matter. Only the soul, and what pertains to it, is truly beautiful; and therefore the beauty of nature is only the reflection of the natural beauty of the spirit—the beautiful has only a spiritual content. But the spiritual must appear in sensuous form. The sensuous manifestation of spirit is only appearance (*Schein*), and this appearance is the only reality of the beautiful. Art is thus the production of this appearance of the Idea, and is a means, together with religion and philosophy, of bringing to consciousness and of expressing the deepest problems of humanity and the highest truths of the spirit.

Truth and beauty, according to Hegel, are one and the same thing, the difference being only that truth is the Idea itself as it exists in itself, and is thinkable. The Idea, manifested externally, becomes to the apprehension not only true but beautiful. The beautiful is the manifestation of the Idea.[23]

Following Hegel came his many adherents, Weisse, Arnold Ruge, Rosenkrantz, Theodor Vischer, and others.

According to Weisse (1801-1867), art is the introduction (*Einbildung*) of the absolute spiritual reality of beauty into external, dead, indifferent matter, and the perception of the latter, apart from the beauty brought into it, presents the negation of all existence in itself (*Negation alles Fürsichseins*).

In the idea of truth, Weisse explains, lies a contradiction between the subjective and the objective sides of knowledge, in that an individual *I* discerns the Universal. This contradiction can be removed by a conception that should unite into one the universal and the individual, which fall asunder in

23 Schasler, pp. 946, 1085, 984 f., 990.

our conceptions of truth. Such a conception would be reconciled (*aufgehoben*) truth. Beauty is such a reconciled truth.[24]

According to Ruge (1802-1880), a strict follower of Hegel, beauty is the Idea expressing itself. The spirit, contemplating itself, either finds itself expressed completely, and then that full expression of itself is beauty, or incompletely, and then it feels the need to alter this imperfect expression of itself and becomes creative art.[25]

According to Vischer (1807-1887), beauty is the Idea in the form of a finite phenomenon. The Idea itself is not indivisible, but forms a system of ideas which may be represented by ascending and descending lines. The higher the idea, the more beauty it contains; but even the lowest contains beauty because it forms an essential link of the system. The highest form of the Idea is personality, and therefore the highest art is that which has for its subject matter the highest personality.[26]

Such were the theories of the German aestheticians in the Hegelian direction, but they did not monopolize aesthetic dissertations. In Germany, side by side and simultaneously with the Hegelian theories, there appeared theories of beauty not only independent of Hegel's position (that beauty is the manifestation of the Idea), but directly contrary to this view, denying and ridiculing it. Such was the line taken by Herbart and, more particularly, by Schopenhauer.

According to Herbart (1776-1841), there is not, and cannot be, any such thing as beauty existing in itself. What does exist is only our opinion, and it is necessary to find the base of this opinion (*Ästhetisches Elementarurteil*). Such bases are connected with our impressions. There are certain relations which we term beautiful, and art consists in finding these relations, which are simultaneous in painting, the plastic art, and architecture, successive and simultaneous in music, and purely successive in poetry. In contradiction to the former aestheticians, Herbart holds that objects are often beautiful which express nothing at all, as, for instance, the rainbow, which is beautiful

---

24 Schasler, pp. 655, 956, 966.   25 Schasler, p. 1017.
26 Schasler, pp. 1097-1100.

for its lines and colors, and not for its mythological connection with Iris or Noah's rainbow.[27]

Another opponent of Hegel was Schopenhauer, who denied Hegel's whole system, his aesthetics included.

According to Schopenhauer (1788-1860), Will objectivizes itself in the world on various planes; and although the higher the plane on which it is objectivized, the more beautiful it is, yet each plane has its own beauty. Renunciation of one's individuality and contemplation of one of these planes of manifestation of Will gives us a perception of beauty. All men, says Schopenhauer, possess the capacity to objectivize the Idea on different planes. The genius of the artist has this capacity in a higher degree and therefore makes a higher beauty manifest.[28]

After these more eminent writers there followed in Germany less original and less influential ones, such as Hartmann, Kirkmann [Reference here is apparently made to Julius Hermann von Kirchmann, 1802-1881, founder of the "Philosophische Bibliothek."—Ed.], Schnasse, and, to some extent, Helmholtz (as an aesthetician), Bergmann, Jungmann, and an innumerable host of others.

According to Hartmann (1842), beauty lies not in the external world or in "the thing in itself"; neither does it reside in the soul of man, but it lies in the "seeming" (*Schein*) produced by the artist. The thing in itself is not beautiful but is transformed into beauty by the artist.[29]

According to Schnasse (1798-1875), there is no perfect beauty in the world. In nature there is only an approach toward it. Art gives what nature cannot give. In the energy of the free ego, conscious of harmony not found in nature, beauty is disclosed.[30]

Kirkmann [i.e., von Kirchmann] wrote on experimental aesthetics. All aspects of history in his system are joined by pure chance. Thus, according to him, there are six realms of

[27] Schasler, pp. 1065 f.   [28] Schasler, pp. 1124, 1107.
[29] Knight, p. 83.   [30] Knight, pp. 81 f.

history: the realm of Knowledge, of Wealth, of Morality, of Faith, of Politics, and of Beauty—and activity in the last-named realm is art.[31]

According to Helmholtz (1821), who wrote on beauty as it relates to music, beauty in musical productions is attained only by following unalterable laws. These laws are not known to the artist, so that beauty is manifested by the artist unconsciously and cannot be subjected to analysis.[32]

According to Bergmann (1840—*Ueber das Schöne,* 1887), to define beauty objectively is impossible. Beauty is perceived only subjectively, and therefore the problem of aesthetics is to define what pleases whom.[33]

According to Jungmann (d. 1885), firstly, beauty is a supra-sensible quality of things; secondly, beauty produces in us pleasure by merely being contemplated; and thirdly, beauty is the foundation of love.[34]

The aesthetic theories of the chief representatives of France, England, and other nations in recent times have been the following:

In France during this period the prominent writers on aesthetics were Cousin, Jouffroy, Pictet, Ravaisson, Lévêque.

Cousin (1792-1867) was an eclectic and a follower of the German idealists. According to his theory, beauty always has a moral foundation. He disputes the doctrine that art is imitation and that the beautiful is what pleases. He affirms that beauty may be defined objectively and that it essentially consists in variety in unity.[35]

After Cousin came Jouffroy (1796-1842), who was a pupil of Cousin's and also a follower of the German aestheticians. According to his definition, beauty is the expression of the invisible by those natural signs which manifest it. The visible world is the garment by means of which we see beauty.[36]

The Swiss writer Pictet repeated Hegel and Plato, supposing

31 Schasler, p. 1121.   32 Knight, pp. 85 f.
33 Knight, p. 88.   34 Knight, p. 116.
35 Knight, pp. 123 f.   36 Knight, p. 88.

beauty to exist in the direct and free manifestation of the divine Idea revealing itself in sense forms.[37]

Lévêque was a follower of Schelling and Hegel. He holds that beauty is something invisible behind nature—a force or spirit revealing itself in ordered energy.[38]

Similar vague opinions about the nature of beauty were expressed by the French metaphysician Ravaisson, who considered beauty to be the ultimate aim and purpose of the world. *"La beauté la plus divine et principalement la plus parfaite contient le secret du monde."* And again, *"Le monde entier est l'oeuvre d'une beauté absolue, qui n'est la cause des choses que par l'amour qu'elle met en elles."* [39]

I purposely abstain from translating these metaphysical expressions, because, however cloudy the Germans may be, the French, once they absorb the theories of the Germans and take to imitating them, far surpass them in uniting heterogeneous conceptions into one expression and putting forward one meaning or another indiscriminately. For instance, the French philosopher Renouvier, when discussing beauty, says, *"Ne craignons pas de dire qu'une vérité qui ne serait pas belle, ne serait qu'un jeu logique de notre esprit et que la seule vérité solide et digne de ce nom c'est la beauté."* [40]

Besides the aesthetic idealists who wrote and still write under the influence of German philosophy, the following recent writers have also influenced the comprehension of art and beauty in France: Taine, Guyau, Cherbuliez, Coster, and Véron.

According to Taine (1828-1893), beauty is the manifesta-

[37] Knight, p. 112.   [38] Knight, pp. 118 f.

[39] ["The most divine and especially the most perfect beauty contains the secret of the world. . . . The whole world is the work of an absolute beauty, which is the cause of things only by the love it puts into them," *La Philosophie en France*, p. 232.—ED.]

[40] ["Let us not be afraid to say that a truth which is not beautiful is only a logical play of our intelligence, and that the only truth that is solid and worthy of the name is beauty," *Du Fondement de l'Induction.*—ED.]

tion of the essential characteristic of any important idea more completely than it is expressed in reality.[41]

Guyau (1854-1888) taught that beauty is not something exterior to the object itself—is not, as it were, a parasitic growth on it—but is itself the very blossoming forth of that on which it appears. Art is the expression of reasonable and conscious life, evoking in us both the deepest consciousness of existence and the highest feelings and loftiest thoughts. Art lifts man from his personal life into the universal life by means not only of participation in the same ideas and beliefs, but also by similarity in feeling.[42]

According to Cherbuliez, art is an activity, (1) satisfying our innate love of forms (*apparences*), (2) endowing these forms with ideas, (3) affording pleasure alike to our senses, heart, and reason. Beauty is not inherent in objects but is an act of our souls. Beauty is an illusion; there is no absolute beauty. But what we consider characteristic and harmonious appears beautiful to us.

Coster held that the ideas of the beautiful, the good, and the true are innate. These ideas illuminate our minds and are identical with God, who is Goodness, Truth, and Beauty. The idea of Beauty includes unity of essence, variety of constitutive elements, and order which brings unity into the various manifestations of life.[43]

For the sake of completeness, I will further cite some of the very latest writings upon art.

La Psychologie du beau et de l'art, by Mario Pilo (1895), says that beauty is a product of our physical feelings. The aim of art is pleasure, but this pleasure (for some reason) he considers to be necessarily highly moral.

The *Essai sur l'art contemporain,* by Fierens Gevaert (1897), says that art rests on its connection with the past and on the religious ideal of the present which the artist holds when giving to his work the form of his individuality.

41 *Philosophie de l'Art,* 1893, I, 47.
42 Knight, pp. 139-141.   43 Knight, p. 134.

Then again, Sar Peladan's *L'art idealiste et mystique* (1894), says that beauty is one of the manifestations of God. "*Il n'y a pas d'autre Réalité que Dieu, il n'y a pas d'autre Vérité que Dieu, il n'y a pas d'autre Beauté que Dieu*" ["There is no other Reality than God, there is no other Truth than God, there is no other Beauty than God," p. 33.—Ed.] This book is very fantastic and very illiterate, but is characteristic in the positions it takes up and noticeable on account of a certain success it is having with the younger generation in France.

All the aesthetics diffused in France up to the present time are similar in kind, but among them Véron's *L'Esthétique* (1878) forms an exception, being reasonable and clear. That work, though it does not give an exact definition of art, at least rids aesthetics of the cloudy conception of an absolute beauty.

According to Véron (1825-1889), art is the manifestation of emotion transmitted externally by a combination of lines, forms, colors, or by a succession of movements, sounds, or words subjected to certain rhythms.[44]

In England, during this period the writers on aesthetics define beauty more and more frequently, not by its own qualities, but by taste, and the discussion about beauty is superseded by a discussion on taste.

After Reid (1704-1796), who acknowledged beauty as being entirely dependent on the spectator, Alison, in his *Essay on the Nature and Principles of Taste* (1790), proved the same thing. From another side this was also asserted by Erasmus Darwin (1731-1802), the grandfather of the celebrated Charles Darwin.

He says that we consider beautiful that which is connected in our conception with what we love. Richard Knight's work, *An Analytical Inquiry into the Principles of Taste,* also tends in the same direction.

Most of the English theories of aesthetics are on the same lines. The prominent writers on aesthetics in England during

[44] *L'Esthétique,* p. 106.

the present century have been Charles Darwin (to some extent), Herbert Spencer, Grant Allen, Ker, and Knight.

According to Charles Darwin (1809-1882—*Descent of Man,* 1871), beauty is a feeling natural not only to man but also to animals, and consequently to the ancestors of man. Birds adorn their nests and esteem beauty in their mates. Beauty has an influence on marriages. Beauty includes a variety of diverse conceptions. The origin of the art of music is the call of the males to the females.[45]

According to Herbert Spencer (b. 1820), the origin of art is play, a thought previously expressed by Schiller. In the lower animals all the energy of life is expended in life-maintenance and race-maintenance; in man, however, there remains, after these needs are satisfied, some superfluous strength. This excess is used in play, which passes over into art. Play is an imitation of real activity; so is art. The sources of aesthetic pleasure are threefold: (1) That "which exercises the faculties affected in the most complete ways, with the fewest drawbacks from exercise," (2) "the difference of a stimulus in large amount which awakens a glow of agreeable feeling," (3) the partial revival of the same, with special combinations.[46]

In Todhunter's *Theory of the Beautiful* (1872), beauty is infinite loveliness, which we apprehend both by reason and by the enthusiasm of love. The recognition of beauty as being such depends on taste; there can be no criterion for it. The only approach to a definition is found in culture. (What culture is, is not defined.) Intrinsically, art—that which affects us through lines, colors, sounds, or words—is not the product of blind forces, but of reasonable ones, working with mutual helpfulness toward a reasonable aim. Beauty is the reconciliation of contradictions.[47]

Grant Allen is a follower of Spencer, and in his *Physiological Aesthetics* (1877) he says that beauty has a physical origin. Aesthetic pleasures come from the contemplation of the beautiful, but the conception of beauty is obtained by a physiologi-

[45] Knight, p. 238.   [46] Knight, pp. 239 f.
[47] Knight, pp. 250-252.

cal process. The origin of art is play; when there is a superfluity of physical strength man gives himself to play; when
there is a superfluity of receptive power man gives himself to
art. The beautiful is that which affords the maximum of
stimulation with the minimum of waste. Differences in the
estimation of beauty proceed from taste. Taste can be educated. We must have faith in the judgments "of the finest-
nurtured and most discriminative" men. These people form
the taste of the next generation.[48]

According to Ker's *Essay on the Philosophy of Art* (1883),
beauty enables us to make part of the objective world intelligible to ourselves without being troubled by reference to other
parts of it, as is inevitable for science. So that art destroys the
opposition between the one and the many, between the law
and its manifestation, between the subject and its object, by
uniting them. Art is the revelation and vindication of freedom because it is free from the darkness and incomprehensibility of finite things.[49]

According to Knight's *Philosophy of the Beautiful*, Part II
(1893), beauty is (as with Schelling) the union of object and
subject, the drawing forth from nature of that which is cog-
nate to man and the recognition in oneself of that which is
common to all nature.

The opinions on beauty and on art here mentioned are far
from exhausting what has been written on the subject. And
every day fresh writers on aesthetics arise in whose disquisi-
tions appear the same enchanted confusion and contradictori-
ness in defining beauty. Some, by inertia, continue the mystical aesthetics of Baumgarten and Hegel with sundry varia-
tions; others transfer the question to the region of subjectivity
and seek for the foundation of the beautiful in questions of
taste; others—the aestheticians of the very latest formation—
seek the origin of beauty in the laws of physiology; and finally,
others again investigate the question quite independently of
the conception of beauty. Thus Sully, in his *Sensation and In-*

48 Knight, pp. 240-243.   49 Knight, pp. 258 f.

tuition: Studies in Psychology and Aesthetics (1874), dismisses the conception of beauty altogether, art, by his definition, being the production of some permanent object or passing action fitted to supply active enjoyment to the producer and a pleasurable impression to a number of spectators or listeners, quite apart from any personal advantage derived from it.[50]

CHAPTER FOUR

To what do these definitions of beauty amount? Not reckoning the thoroughly inaccurate definitions of beauty which fail to cover the conception of art, and which suppose beauty to consist either in utility or in adjustment to a purpose, or in symmetry, or in order, or in proportion, or in smoothness, or in harmony of the parts, or in unity amid variety, or in various combinations of these—not reckoning these unsatisfactory attempts at objective definition, all the aesthetic definitions of beauty lead to two fundamental conceptions. The first is that beauty is something having an independent existence (existing in itself), that it is one of the manifestations of the absolutely Perfect, of the Idea, of the Spirit, of Will, or of God; the other is that beauty is a kind of pleasure we receive which does not have personal advantage for its object.

The first of these definitions was accepted by Fichte, Schelling, Hegel, Schopenhauer, and the philosophizing Frenchmen Cousin, Jouffroy, Ravaisson, and others, not to enumerate the second-rate aesthetic philosophers. And this same objective-mystical definition of beauty is held by a majority of the educated people of our day. It is a conception very widely spread, especially among the elder generation.

The second view, that beauty is a certain kind of pleasure we receive which does not have personal advantage for its aim,

[50] Knight, p. 243.

finds favor chiefly among the English aesthetic writers and is shared by the other part of our society, principally by the younger generation.

So there are (and it could not be otherwise) only two definitions of beauty: the one objective, mystical, merging this conception into that of the highest perfection, God—a fantastic definition, founded on nothing; the other, on the contrary, a very simple and intelligible subjective one, which considers beauty to be that which pleases (I do not add to the word "pleases" the words "without the aim of advantage," because "pleases" naturally presupposes the absence of the idea of profit).

On the one hand, beauty is viewed as something mystical and very elevated, but unfortunately at the same time very indefinite and, consequently, embracing philosophy, religion, and life itself (as in the theories of Schelling and Hegel and their German and French followers); or, on the other hand (as necessarily follows from the definition of Kant and his adherents), beauty is simply a certain kind of disinterested pleasure received by us. And this conception of beauty, although it seems very clear, is, unfortunately, again inexact, for it widens out on the other side; i.e., it includes the pleasure derived from drink, from food, from touching a delicate skin, etc., as is acknowledged by Guyau, Kralik, and others.

It is true that, following the development of the aesthetic doctrines on beauty, we may notice that, though at first (in the times when the foundations of the science of aesthetics were being laid) the metaphysical definition of beauty prevailed, yet the nearer we get to our own times, the more does an experimental definition (recently assuming a physiological form) come to the front, so that at last we even meet with such aestheticians as Véron and Sully who try to escape entirely from the conception of beauty. But such aestheticians have very little success, and with the majority of the public, as well as of artists and the learned, a conception of beauty is firmly held which agrees with the definitions contained in most of the aesthetic treatises, i.e., which regards beauty either as something mystical or metaphysical or as a special kind of enjoyment.

What, then, is this conception of beauty so stubbornly held to by people of our circle and day as furnishing a definition of art?

In the subjective aspect, we call beauty that which supplies us with a particular kind of pleasure.

In the objective aspect, we call beauty something absolutely perfect, and we acknowledge it to be so only because we receive, from the manifestation of this absolute perfection, a certain kind of pleasure; so this objective definition is nothing but the subjective conception differently expressed. In reality both conceptions of beauty amount to one and the same thing —namely, the reception by us of a certain kind of pleasure; i.e., we call "beauty" that which pleases us without evoking in us desire.

Such being the position of affairs, it would seem only natural that the science of art should decline to content itself with a definition of art based on beauty (i.e., on that which pleases), and seek a general definition which should apply to all artistic productions, and by reference to which we might decide whether a certain article belonged to the realm of art or not. But no such definition is supplied, as the reader may see from those summaries of the aesthetic theories which I have given, and as he may discover even more clearly from the original aesthetic works if he will be at the pains to read them. All attempts to define absolute beauty in itself—whether as an imitation of nature, or as suitability to its object, or as a correspondence of parts, or as symmetry, or as harmony, or as unity in variety, etc.—either define nothing at all or define only some traits of some artistic productions and are far from including all that everybody has always held, and still holds, to be art.

There is no objective definition of beauty. The existing definitions (both the metaphysical and the experimental) amount only to one and the same subjective definition, which (strange as it seems to say so) is that art is that which makes beauty manifest, and beauty is that which pleases (without exciting desire). Many aestheticians have felt the insufficiency and instability of such a definition, and, in order to give it a firm basis, have asked themselves why a thing pleases. And they have converted the discussion on beauty into a question concerning taste, as did Hutcheson, Voltaire, Diderot, and others. But all attempts to define what taste is must lead to nothing, as the reader may see both from the history of aesthetics and experimentally. There is and can be no explanation of why one thing pleases one man and displeases another, or vice versa. So that the whole existing science of aesthetics fails to do what we might expect from it, being a mental activity calling itself a science; namely, it does not define the qualities and laws of art or of the beautiful (if that be the content of art), or the nature of taste (if taste decides the question of art and its merit), and then, on the basis of such definitions, acknowledge as art those productions which correspond to these laws and reject those which do not come under them. But this science of aesthetics consists in first acknowledging a certain set of productions to be art (because they please us), and then framing such a theory of art that all those productions which please a certain circle of people should fit into it. There exists an art canon according to which certain productions favored by our circle are acknowledged as being art—Phidias, Sophocles, Homer, Titian, Raphael, Bach, Beethoven, Dante, Shakespeare, Goethe, and others—and the aesthetic laws must be such as to embrace all these productions. In aesthetic literature you will incessantly meet with opinions on the merit and importance of art, founded not on any certain laws by which this or that is held to be good or bad, but merely on the consideration whether this art tallies with the art canon we have drawn up.

The other day I was reading a far from ill-written book by Folgeldt. Discussing the demand for morality in works of art, the author plainly says that we must not demand morality in art. And in proof of this he advances the fact that if we admit such a demand, Shakespeare's *Romeo and Juliet* and

Goethe's *Wilhelm Meister* would not fit into the definition of good art; but since both these books are included in our canon of art, he concludes that the demand is unjust. And therefore it is necessary to find a definition of art which shall fit the works; and instead of a demand for morality, Folgeldt postulates as the basis of art a demand for the important (*das Bedeutungsvolle*).

All the existing aesthetic standards are built on this plan. Instead of giving a definition of true art and then deciding what is and what is not good art by judging whether a work conforms or does not conform to the definition, a certain class of works which for some reason please a certain circle of people is accepted as being art, and a definition of art is then devised to cover all these productions. I recently came upon a remarkable instance of this method in a very good German work, *The History of Art in the Nineteenth Century,* by Muther. Describing the pre-Raphaelites, the Decadents and the Symbolists (who are already included in the canon of art), he not only does not venture to blame their tendency, but earnestly endeavors to widen his standard so that it may include them all, they appearing to him to represent a legitimate reaction from the excesses of realism. No matter what insanities appear in art, when once they find acceptance among the upper classes of our society a theory is quickly invented to explain and sanction them, just as if there had never been periods in history when certain special circles of people recognized and approved false, deformed, and insensate art which subsequently left no trace and has been utterly forgotten. And to what lengths the insanity and deformity of art may go, especially when, as in our days, it knows that it is considered infallible, may be seen by what is being done in the art of our circle today.

So the theory of art founded on beauty, expounded by aesthetics, and in dim outline professed by the public, is nothing but the setting up as good of that which has pleased and pleases us, i.e., pleases a certain class of people.

In order to define any human activity it is necessary to understand its sense and importance. And in order to do that it is primarily necessary to examine that activity in itself, in its dependence on its causes and in connection with its effects, and not merely in relation to the pleasure we can get from it.

If we say that the aim of any activity is merely our pleasure, and define it solely by that pleasure, our definition will evidently be a false one. But this is precisely what has occurred in the efforts to define art. Now, if we consider the food question it will not occur to anyone to affirm that the importance of food consists in the pleasure we receive when eating it. Everyone understands that the satisfaction of our taste cannot serve as a basis for our definition of the merits of food, and that we have therefore no right to presuppose that the dinners with cayenne pepper, Limburg cheese, alcohol, etc., to which we are accustomed and which please us, form the very best human food.

And in the same way, beauty, or that which pleases us, can in no sense serve as the basis for the definition of art; nor can a series of objects which afford us pleasure serve as the model of what art should be.

To see the aim and purpose of art in the pleasure we get from it is like assuming (as is done by people of the lowest moral development, e.g., by savages) that the purpose and aim of food is the pleasure derived when consuming it.

Just as people who conceive the aim and purpose of food to be pleasure cannot recognize the real meaning of eating, so people who consider the aim of art to be pleasure cannot realize its true meaning and purpose because they attribute to an activity the meaning of which lies in its connection with other phenomena of life, the false and exceptional aim of pleasure. People come to understand that the meaning of eating lies in the nourishment of the body only when they cease to consider that the object of that activity is pleasure. And it is the same with regard to art. People will come to understand the meaning of art only when they cease to consider that the aim of that activity is beauty, i.e., pleasure. The acknowledgment of beauty (i.e., of a certain kind of pleasure received from art) as being the aim of art not only fails to assist us in finding a definition of what art is, but, on the contrary, by transferring the question into a region quite foreign to art (into metaphysical, psychological, physiological, and even historical discussions as to why such a production pleases one person, and such another displeases or pleases someone else), it renders such definition impossible. And since discussions as to why one man likes pears and another prefers meat do not help toward finding a definition of what is essential in nourishment, so the solution of questions of taste in art (to which the discussions on art involuntarily come) not only does not help to make clear in what this particular human activity which we call art really consists, but renders such elucidation quite impossible until we rid ourselves of a conception which justifies every kind of art at the cost of confusing the whole matter.

To the question, what is this art to which is offered up the labor of millions, the very lives of men, and even morality itself? we have extracted replies from the existing aesthetics, which all amount to this: that the aim of art is beauty, that beauty is recognized by the enjoyment it gives, and that artistic enjoyment is a good and important thing because it *is* enjoyment. In a word, enjoyment is good because it is enjoyment. Thus what is considered the definition of art is no definition at all, but only a shuffle to justify existing art. Therefore, however strange it may seem to say so, in spite of the mountains of books written about art no exact definition of art has been constructed. And the reason for this is that the conception of art has been based on the conception of beauty.

CHAPTER FIVE

WHAT is art—if we put aside the conception of beauty, which confuses the whole matter? The latest and most comprehensible definitions of art, apart from the conception of beauty, are the following: (1) Art is an activity arising even in the animal kingdom, *a*, springing from sexual desire and the propensity to play (Schiller, Darwin, Spencer), and *b*, accompanied by a pleasurable excitement of the nervous system (Grant Allen). This is the physiological-evolutionary definition. (2) Art is the external manifestation by means of lines, colors, movements, sounds, or words, of emotions felt by man (Véron). This is the experimental definition. According to the very latest definition, (3) Art is "the production of some permanent object or passing action, which is fitted, not only to supply an active enjoyment to the producer, but to convey a pleasurable impression to a number of spectators or listeners, quite apart from any personal advantage to be derived from it" (Sully).

Notwithstanding the superiority of these definitions to the metaphysical definitions which depended on the conception of beauty, they are yet far from exact. The first, the physiological-evolutionary definition (1*a*), is inexact because, instead of speaking about the artistic activity itself, which is the real matter in hand, it treats of the derivation of art. The modification of it (1*b*), based on the physiological effects on the human organism, is inexact because within the limits of such definition many other human activities can be included, as has occurred in the neo-aesthetic theories, which reckon as art the preparation of handsome clothes, pleasant scents, and even victuals.

The experimental definition (2), which makes art consist in the expression of emotions, is inexact because a man may express his emotions by means of lines, colors, sounds, or words, and yet may not act on others by such expression, and then the manifestation of his emotions is not art.

The third definition (that of Sully) is inexact because in the production of objects or actions affording pleasure to the producer and a pleasant emotion to the spectators or hearers, apart from personal advantage, may be included the showing of conjuring tricks or gymnastic exercises and other activities which are not art. And further, many things, the production of which does not afford pleasure to the producer and the sensation received from which is unpleasant, such as gloomy, heartrending scenes in a poetic description or a play, may nevertheless be undoubted works of art.

The inaccuracy of all these definitions arises from the fact that in them all (as also in the metaphysical definitions) the object considered is the pleasure art may give, and not the purpose it may serve in the life of man and of humanity.

In order correctly to define art, it is necessary, first of all, to cease to consider it as a means to pleasure and to consider it as one of the conditions of human life. Viewing it in this way we cannot fail to observe that art is one of the means of intercourse between man and man.

Every work of art causes the receiver to enter into a certain kind of relationship both with him who produced, or is producing, the art, and with all those who, simultaneously, previously, or subsequently, receive the same artistic impression.

Speech, transmitting the thoughts and experiences of men, serves as a means of union among them, and art acts in a similar manner. The peculiarity of this latter means of intercourse, distinguishing it from intercourse by means of words, consists in this, that whereas by words a man transmits his thoughts to another, by means of art he transmits his feelings.

The activity of art is based on the fact that a man, receiving through his sense of hearing or sight another man's expression of feeling, is capable of experiencing the emotion which moved the man who expressed it. To take the simplest example: one man laughs, and another who hears becomes merry; or a man weeps, and another who hears feels sorrow. A man is excited or irritated, and another man seeing him comes to a similar state of mind. By his movements or by the sounds of his voice, a man expresses courage and determination or sadness and calmness, and this state of mind passes on to others. A man suffers, expressing his sufferings by groans and spasms, and this suffering transmits itself to other people; a man expresses his feeling of admiration, devotion, fear, respect, or love to certain objects, persons, or phenomena, and others are infected by the same feelings of admiration, devotion, fear, respect, or love to the same objects, persons, and phenomena.

And it is upon this capacity of man to receive another man's expression of feeling and experience those feelings himself, that the activity of art is based.

If a man infects another or others directly, immediately, by his appearance or by the sounds he gives vent to at the very time he experiences the feeling; if he causes another man to yawn when he himself cannot help yawning, or to laugh or cry when he himself is obliged to laugh or cry, or to suffer when he himself is suffering—that does not amount to art.

Art begins when one person, with the object of joining another or others to himself in one and the same feeling, expresses that feeling by certain external indications. To take the simplest example: a boy, having experienced, let us say, fear on encountering a wolf, relates that encounter; and, in order to evoke in others the feeling he has experienced, describes himself, his condition before the encounter, the surroundings, the wood, his own lightheartedness, and then the wolf's appearance, its movements, the distance between himself and the wolf, etc. All this, if only the boy, when telling the story, again experiences the feelings he had lived through and infects the hearers and compels them to feel what the narrator had experienced, is art. If even the boy had not seen a wolf but had frequently been afraid of one, and if, wishing to evoke in others the fear he had felt, he invented an encounter with a wolf and recounted it so as to make his hearers share the feelings he experienced when he feared the wolf, that also would be art. And just in the same way it is art if a man, having experienced either the fear of suffering or the attraction of enjoyment (whether in reality or in imagination), expresses these feelings on canvas or in marble so that others are infected by them. And it is also art if a man feels or imagines to himself feelings of delight, gladness, sorrow, despair, courage, or despondency and the transition from one to another of these feelings, and expresses these feelings by sounds so that the hearers are infected by them and experience them as they were experienced by the composer.

The feelings with which the artist infects others may be most various—very strong or very weak, very important or very insignificant, very bad or very good: feelings of love for one's own country, self-devotion and submission to fate or to God expressed in a drama, raptures of lovers described in a novel, feelings of voluptuousness expressed in a picture, courage expressed in a triumphal march, merriment evoked by a dance, humor evoked by a funny story, the feeling of quietness transmitted by an evening landscape or by a lullaby, or the feeling of admiration evoked by a beautiful arabesque—it is all art.

If only the spectators or auditors are infected by the feelings which the author has felt, it is art.

To evoke in oneself a feeling one has once experienced, and having evoked it in oneself, then, by means of movements, lines, colors, sounds, or forms expressed in words, so to transmit that feeling that others may experience the same feeling—this is the activity of art.

Art is a human activity consisting in this, that one man consciously, by means of certain external signs, hands on to others feelings he has lived through, and that other people are infected by these feelings and also experience them.

Art is not, as the metaphysicians say, the manifestation of some mysterious Idea of beauty or God; it is not, as the aesthetical physiologists say, a game in which man lets off his excess of stored-up energy; it is not the expression of man's emotions by external signs; it is not the production of pleasing objects; and, above all, it is not pleasure; but it is a means of union among men, joining them together in the same feelings, and indispensable for the life and progress toward well-being of individuals and of humanity.

As, thanks to man's capacity to express thoughts by words, every man may know all that has been done for him in the realms of thought by all humanity before his day, and can in the present, thanks to this capacity to understand the thoughts of others, become a sharer in their activity and can himself hand on to his contemporaries and descendants the thoughts he has assimilated from others, as well as those which have arisen within himself; so, thanks to man's capacity to be infected with the feelings of others by means of art, all that is being lived through by his contemporaries is accessible to him, as well as the feelings experienced by men thousands of years ago, and he has also the possibility of transmitting his own feelings to others.

If people lacked this capacity to receive the thoughts conceived by the men who preceded them and to pass on to others their own thoughts, men would be like wild beasts, or like Kaspar Hauser.[1]

And if men lacked this other capacity of being infected by art, people might be almost more savage still, and, above all, more separated from, and more hostile to, one another.

And therefore the activity of art is a most important one, as important as the activity of speech itself and as generally diffused.

We are accustomed to understand art to be only what we hear and see in theaters, concerts, and exhibitions, together with buildings, statues, poems, novels. . . . But all this is but the smallest part of the art by which we communicate with each other in life. All human life is filled with works of art of every kind—from cradlesong, jest, mimicry, the ornamenta-

1 "The foundling of Nuremberg," found in the market-place of that town on May 26, 1828, apparently some sixteen years old. He spoke little and was almost totally ignorant even of common objects. He subsequently explained that he had been brought up in confinement underground and visited by only one man, whom he seldom saw.—TR.

tion of houses, dress, and utensils, up to church services, buildings, monuments, and triumphal processions. It is all artistic activity. So that by art, in the limited sense of the word, we do not mean all human activity transmitting feelings, but only that part which we for some reason select from it and to which we attach special importance.

This special importance has always been given by all men to that part of this activity which transmits feelings flowing from their religious perception, and this small part of art they have specifically called art, attaching to it the full meaning of the word.

That was how men of old—Socrates, Plato, and Aristotle—looked on art. Thus did the Hebrew prophets and the ancient Christians regard art; thus it was, and still is, understood by the Mohammedans, and thus it still is understood by religious folk among our own peasantry.

Some teachers of mankind—as Plato in his *Republic* and people such as the primitive Christians, the strict Mohammedans, and the Buddhists—have gone so far as to repudiate all art.

People viewing art in this way (in contradiction to the prevalent view of today which regards any art as good if only it affords pleasure) considered, and consider, that art (as contrasted with speech, which need not be listened to) is so highly dangerous in its power to infect people against their wills that mankind will lose far less by banishing all art than by tolerating each and every art.

Evidently such people were wrong in repudiating all art, for they denied that which cannot be denied—one of the indispensable means of communication, without which mankind could not exist. But not less wrong are the people of civilized European society of our class and day in favoring any art if it but serves beauty, i.e., gives people pleasure.

Formerly people feared lest among the works of art there might chance to be some causing corruption, and they prohibited art altogether. Now they only fear lest they should be deprived of any enjoyment art can afford, and patronize any art. And I think the last error is much grosser than the first and that its consequences are far more harmful.

CHAPTER SIX

B UT how could it happen that that very art, which in ancient times was merely tolerated (if tolerated at all), should have come in our times to be invariably considered a good thing if only it affords pleasure?

It has resulted from the following causes. The estimation of the value of art (i.e., of the feelings it transmits) depends on men's perception of the meaning of life, depends on what they consider to be the good and the evil of life. And what is good and what is evil is defined by what are termed religions.

Humanity unceasingly moves forward from a lower, more partial and obscure understanding of life to one more general and more lucid. And in this, as in every movement, there are leaders—those who have understood the meaning of life more clearly than others—and of these advanced men there is always one who has in his words and by his life expressed this meaning more clearly, accessibly, and strongly than others. This man's expression of the meaning of life, together with those superstitions, traditions, and ceremonies which usually form themselves round the memory of such a man, is what is called a religion. Religions are the exponents of the highest comprehension of life accessible to the best and foremost men at a given time in a given society—a comprehension toward which, inevitably and irresistibly, all the rest of that society must advance. And therefore only religions have always served, and still serve, as bases for the valuation of human sentiments. If feelings bring men nearer the ideal their religion indicates, if they are in harmony with it and do not contradict it, they are good; if they estrange men from it and oppose it, they are bad.

If the religion places the meaning of life in worshiping one God and fulfilling what is regarded as His will, as was the case among the Jews, then the feelings flowing from love to that God and to His law successfully transmitted through the art of poetry by the prophets, by the psalms, or by the epic of the book of Genesis, is good, high art. All opposing that, as for instance the transmission of feelings of devotion to strange gods or of feelings incompatible with the law of God, would be considered bad art. Or if, as was the case among the Greeks, the religion places the meaning of life in earthly happiness, in beauty and in strength, then art successfully transmitting the joy and energy of life would be considered good art, but art which transmitted feelings of effeminacy or despondency would be bad art. If the meaning of life is seen in the well-being of one's nation or in honoring one's ancestors and continuing the mode of life led by them, as was the case among the Romans and the Chinese respectively, then art transmitting feelings of joy at sacrificing one's personal well-being for the common weal, or at exalting one's ancestors and maintaining their traditions, would be considered good art, but art expressing feelings contrary to this would be regarded as bad. If the meaning of life is seen in freeing oneself from the yoke of animalism, as is the case among the Buddhists, then art successfully transmitting feelings that elevate the soul and humble the flesh will be good art, and all that transmits feelings strengthening the bodily passions will be bad art.

In every age and in every human society there exists a religious sense, common to that whole society, of what is good and what is bad, and it is this religious conception that decides the value of the feelings transmitted by art. And therefore, among all nations art which transmitted feelings considered to be good by this general religious sense was recognized as being good and was encouraged, but art which transmitted feelings considered to be bad by this general religious conception was recognized as being bad, and was rejected. All the rest of the immense field of art by means of which people communicate one with another was not esteemed at all, and

was only noticed when it ran counter to the religious conception of its age, and then merely to be repudiated. Thus it was
among all nations—Greeks, Jews, Indians, Egyptians, and
Chinese—and so it was when Christianity appeared.

The Christianity of the first centuries recognized as productions of good art only legends, lives of saints, sermons,
prayers, and hymn singing, evoking love of Christ, emotion at
His life, desire to follow His example, renunciation of worldly
life, humility, and the love of others. All productions transmitting feelings of personal enjoyment they considered to be
bad and therefore rejected; for instance, tolerating plastic
representations only when they were symbolical, they rejected
all the pagan sculptures.

This was so among the Christians of the first centuries who
accepted Christ's teaching, if not quite in its true form, at
least not in the perverted, paganized form in which it was
accepted subsequently.

But besides this Christianity, from the time of the wholesale conversion of nations by order of the authorities, as in
the days of Constantine, Charlemagne, and Vladimir, there
appeared another, a Church Christianity, which was nearer
to paganism than to Christ's teaching. And thus Church
Christianity, in accordance with its own teaching, estimated
quite otherwise the feelings of people and the productions of
art which transmitted those feelings.

This Church Christianity not only did not acknowledge the
fundamental and essential positions of true Christianity—the
immediate relationship of each man to the Father, the consequent brotherhood and equality of all men, and the substitution of humility and love in place of every kind of
violence—but on the contrary, having set up a heavenly hierarchy similar to the pagan mythology, and having introduced
the worship of Christ, of the Virgin, of angels, of apostles, of
saints, and of martyrs, and not only of these divinities themselves but also of their images, it made blind faith in the
Church and its ordinances the essential point of its teaching.

However foreign this teaching may have been to true

Christianity, however degraded, not only in comparison with true Christianity, but even with the life-conception of Romans such as Julian and others—it was, for all that, to the barbarians who accepted it a higher doctrine than their former adoration of gods, heroes, and good and bad spirits. And therefore this teaching was a religion to them, and on the basis of that religion the art of the time was assessed. And art transmitting pious adoration of the Virgin, Jesus, the saints, and the angels, a blind faith in and submission to the Church, fear of torments and hope of blessedness in a life beyond the grave, was considered good; all art opposed to this was considered bad.

The teaching on the basis of which this art arose was a perversion of Christ's teaching, but the art which sprang up on this perverted teaching was nevertheless a true art because it corresponded to the religious view of life held by the people among whom it arose.

The artists of the Middle Ages, vitalized by the same source of feeling—religion—as the mass of the people, and transmitting in architecture, sculpture, painting, music, poetry, or drama the feelings and states of mind they experienced, were true artists; and their activity, founded on the highest conceptions accessible to their age and common to the entire people, though for our times a mean art, was nevertheless a true one, shared by the whole community.

And this was the state of things until in the upper, rich, more educated classes of European society doubt arose as to the truth of that understanding of life which was expressed by Church Christianity. When, after the Crusades and the maximum development of papal power and its abuses, people of the rich classes became acquainted with the wisdom of the classics and saw, on the one hand, the reasonable lucidity of the teaching of the ancient sages, and, on the other hand, the incompatibility of the Church doctrine with the teaching of Christ, they found it impossible for them to continue to believe the Church teaching.

If in externals they still kept to the forms of Church teaching, they could no longer believe in it and held to it only by inertia and for the sake of influencing the masses, who continued to believe blindly in Church doctrine and whom the upper classes, for their own advantage, considered it necessary to support in those beliefs.

So a time came when Church Christianity ceased to be the general religious doctrine of all Christian people; some—the masses—continued blindly to believe in it, but the upper classes—those in whose hands lay the power and wealth, and therefore the leisure to produce art and the means to stimulate it—ceased to believe in that teaching.

In respect to religion, the upper circles of the Middle Ages found themselves in the same position in which the educated Romans were before Christianity arose, i.e., they no longer believed in the religion of the masses, but had no beliefs to put in place of the worn-out Church doctrine which for them had lost its meaning.

There was only this difference: that whereas for the Romans who lost faith in their emperor-gods and household-gods it was impossible to extract anything further from all the complex mythology they had borrowed from all the conquered nations, and it was consequently necessary to find a completely new conception of life, the people of the Middle Ages, when they doubted the truth of the Church teaching, had no need to seek a fresh one. That Christian teaching which they professed in a perverted form as Church doctrine had mapped out the path of human progress so far ahead that they had but to rid themselves of those perversions which hid the teaching announced by Christ and to adopt its real meaning—if not completely, then at least in some greater degree than that in which the Church had held it. And this was partially done, not only in the reformations of Wycliff, Huss, Luther, and Calvin, but by all that current of non-Church Christianity represented in earlier times by the Paulicians, the Bogomili,[1] and afterward by the Waldenses and the other non-Church

[1] Eastern sects well known in early Church history, who rejected the Church's rendering of Christ's teaching and were cruelly persecuted.—Tr.

Christians who were called heretics. But this could be, and was, done chiefly by poor people—who did not rule. A few of the rich and strong, like Francis of Assisi and others, accepted the Christian teaching in its full significance, even though it undermined their privileged positions. But most people of the upper classes (though in the depth of their souls they had lost faith in the Church teaching) could not or would not act thus, because the essence of that Christian view of life, which stood ready to be adopted when once they rejected the Church faith, was a teaching of the brotherhood (and therefore the equality) of man, and this did not support those privileges on which they lived, in which they had grown up and been educated, and to which they were accustomed. Not in the depth of their hearts believing in the Church teaching—which had outlived its age and had no longer any true meaning for them—and not being strong enough to accept true Christianity, men of these rich, governing classes—popes, kings, dukes, and all the great ones of the earth—were left without any religion, with but the external forms of one which they supported as being profitable and even necessary for themselves, since these forms screened a teaching which justified those privileges which they made use of. In reality these people believed in nothing, just as the Romans of the first centuries of our era believed in nothing. But at the same time these were the people who had the power and the wealth, and these were the people who rewarded art and directed it.

And, let it be noticed, it was just among these people that there grew up an art esteemed, not according to its success in expressing men's religious feelings, but in proportion to its beauty—in other words, according to the enjoyment it gave.

No longer able to believe in the Church religion, whose falsehood they had detected, and incapable of accepting true Christian teaching, which denounced their whole manner of life, these rich and powerful people, stranded without any religious conception of life, involuntarily returned to that pagan view of things which places life's meaning in personal enjoyment. And then took place among the upper classes what is called the "Renaissance of science and art," and which was really not only a denial of every religion, but also an assertion that religion is unnecessary.

The Church doctrine is so coherent a system that it cannot be altered or corrected without destroying it altogether. As soon as doubt arose with regard to the infallibility of the Pope (and this doubt was then in the minds of all educated people), doubt inevitably followed as to the truth of tradition. But doubt as to the truth of tradition is fatal not only to popery and Catholicism, but also to the whole Church creed with all its dogmas: the divinity of Christ, the resurrection, and the Trinity; and it destroys the authority of the Scriptures, since they were considered to be inspired only because the tradition of the Church decided it so.

So the majority of the highest classes of that age, even the popes and the ecclesiastics, really believed in nothing at all. In the Church doctrine these people did not believe, for they saw its insolvency; but neither could they follow Francis of Assisi, Keltchitsky,[2] and most of the heretics, in acknowledging the moral, social teaching of Christ, for that teaching undermined their social position. And so these people remained without any religious view of life. And, having none, they could have no standard wherewith to estimate what was good and what was bad art but that of personal enjoyment. And, having acknowledged their criterion of what was good to be pleasure, i.e., beauty, these people of the upper classes of European society went back in their comprehension of art to the gross conception of the primitive Greeks which Plato had already condemned. And comformably to this understanding of life, a theory of art was formulated.

[2] Keltchitsky, a Bohemian of the fifteenth century, was the author of a remarkable book, *The Net of Faith*, directed against Church and State. It is mentioned in Tolstoy's *The Kingdom of God is Within You.*—TR.

CHAPTER SEVEN

FROM the time that people of the upper classes lost faith in Church Christianity, beauty (i.e., the pleasure received from art) became their standard of good and bad art. And in accordance with that view, an aesthetic theory naturally sprang up among those upper classes justifying such a conception—a theory according to which the aim of art is to exhibit beauty. The partisans of this aesthetic theory, in confirmation of its truth, affirmed that it was no invention of their own, but that it existed in the nature of things and was recognized even by the ancient Greeks. But this assertion was quite arbitrary and has no foundation other than the fact that among the ancient Greeks, in consequence of the low grade of their moral ideal (as compared with the Christian), their conception of the good, τὸ ἀγαθόν, was not yet sharply divided from their conception of the beautiful, τὸ καλόν.

That highest perfection of goodness (not only not identical with beauty, but, for the most part, contrasting with it) which was discerned by the Jews even in the times of Isaiah and fully expressed by Christianity, was quite unknown to the Greeks. They supposed that the beautiful must necessarily also be the good. It is true that their foremost thinkers—Socrates, Plato, Aristotle—felt that goodness may happen not to coincide with beauty. Socrates expressly subordinated beauty to goodness; Plato, to unite the two conceptions, spoke of spiritual beauty, while Aristotle demanded from art that it should have a moral influence on people (κάθαρσις [1]). But, notwithstanding all this, they could not quite dismiss the notion that beauty and goodness coincide.

And consequently, in the language of that period a compound word (καλο-κἀγαθία, beauty-goodness) came into use to express that notion.

Evidently the Greek sages began to draw near to that perception of goodness which is expressed in Buddhism and in

1 [Katharsis. Cf. Aristotle, *On the Art of Poetry.*—ED.]

Christianity, and they got entangled in defining the relation
between goodness and beauty. Plato's reasonings about beauty
and goodness are full of contradictions. And it was just this
confusion of ideas that those Europeans of a later age, who
had lost all faith, tried to elevate into a law. They tried to
prove that this union of beauty and goodness is inherent in
the very essence of things, that beauty and goodness must coincide, and that the word and conception καλο-κἀγαθία (which
had a meaning for Greeks, but has none at all for Christians)
represents the highest ideal of humanity. On this misunder-
standing the new science of aesthetics was built up. And to
justify its existence, the teachings of the ancients on art were
so twisted as to make it appear that this invented science of
aesthetics had existed among the Greeks.

In reality, the reasoning of the ancients on art was quite
unlike ours. As Benard in his book on the aesthetics of Aristotle quite justly remarks:

> Pour qui veut y regarder de près, la théorie du beau et celle
> de l'art sont tout à fait séparées dans Aristote, comme elles
> le sont dans Platon et chez tous leurs successeurs (L'Esthé-
> tique d'Aristote et de ses Successeurs, Paris, 1889, p. 28).[2]

And indeed the reasoning of the ancients on art not only
does not confirm our science of aesthetics, but rather contra-
dicts its doctrine of beauty. But nevertheless all the aesthetic
guides, from Schasler to Knight, declare that the science of
the beautiful—aesthetic science—was initiated by the ancients,
by Socrates, Plato, Aristotle; and was continued, they say, partially by the Epicureans and Stoics: by Seneca and Plutarch,
down to Plotinus. But it is supposed that this science by some
unfortunate accident suddenly vanished in the fourth century
and stayed away for about 1500 years, and only after these
1500 years had passed did it revive in Germany, 1750 A.D., in
Baumgarten's doctrine.

[2] Anyone examining closely may see that the theory of beauty and that
of art are quite separated in Aristotle as they are in Plato and in all their
successors.

After Plotinus, says Schasler, fifteen centuries passed away during which there was not the slightest scientific interest felt for the world of beauty and art. These one and a half thousand years, says he, have been lost to aesthetics and have contributed nothing toward the erection of the learned edifice of this science.[3]

3 Die Lücke von fünf Jahrhunderten, welche zwischen den kunstphilosophischen Betrachtungen des Plato und Aristoteles und die des Plotins fällt, kann zwar auffällig erscheinen; dennoch kann man eigentlich nicht sagen, dass in dieser Zwischenzeit überhaupt von ästhetischen Dingen nicht die Rede gewesen; oder dass gar ein völliger Mangel an Zusammenhang zwischen den Kunstanschauungen des letztgenannten Philosophen und denen der ersteren existiere. Freilich wurde die von Aristoteles begründete Wissenschaft in Nichts dadurch gefördert; immerhin aber zeigt sich in jener Zwischenzeit noch ein gewisses Interesse für ästhetische Fragen. Nach Plotin aber, die wenigen, ihm in der Zeit nahestehenden Philosophen, wie Longin, Augustin, u. s. f. kommen, wie wir gesehen, kaum in Betracht und schliessen sich übrigens in ihrer Anschauungsweise an ihn an,—vergehen nicht fünf, sondern *fünfzehn Fahrhunderte,* in denen von irgend einem wissenschaftlichen Interesse für die Welt des Schönen und der Kunst nichts zu spüren ist.

Diese anderthalbtausend Jahre, innerhalb deren der Weltgeist durch die mannigfachsten Kämpfe hindurch zu einer völlig neuen Gestaltung des Lebens sich durcharbeitete, sind für die Aesthetik, hinsichtlich des weiteren Ausbaus dieser Wissenschaft verloren.—MAX SCHASLER. [*Op. cit.,* p. 253.]

[The gap of five centuries which lies between the observations of Plato and Aristole on art and those of Plotinus may initially seem striking. One cannot say, however, that during this period no work in aesthetics was done, or that there existed a complete lack of correspondence between the theories of art of the former philosophers and that of the latter. Although it must be admitted that the science which Aristotle had founded was not advanced in any respect, during this interval a certain interest in aesthetic problems did remain alive. But after Plotinus, if we disregard the few philosophers close to him in time such as Longinus, Augustine, and others, who follow him in their theories and hardly come into question, there passed not five but fifteen centuries in which there was no trace of a scientific interest in the world of the beautiful and of art.

These one-and-a-half thousand years, during which the Weltgeist, with manifold struggles, worked toward a completely new form of life, are lost as far as the further development of the science of aesthetics is concerned.—Ed.]

In reality nothing of the kind happened. The science of aesthetics, the science of the beautiful, neither did nor could vanish, because it never existed. Simply, the Greeks (just like everybody else, always and everywhere) considered art (like everything else) good only when it served goodness (as they understood goodness), and bad when it was in opposition to that goodness. And the Greeks themselves were so little developed morally that goodness and beauty seemed to them to coincide. On that obsolete Greek view of life was erected the science of aesthetics, invented by men of the eighteenth century and especially shaped and mounted in Baumgarten's theory. The Greeks (as any one may see who will read Benard's admirable book on Aristotle and his successors and Walter's work on Plato) never had a science of aesthetics.

Aesthetic theories arose about one hundred and fifty years ago among the wealthy classes of the Christian European world, and arose simultaneously among different nations— German, Italian, Dutch, French, and English. The founder and organizer of it, who gave it a scientific, theoretic form, was Baumgarten.

With a characteristically German external exactitude, pedantry, and symmetry, he devised and expounded this extraordinary theory. And, notwithstanding its obvious insolidity, nobody else's theory so pleased the cultured crowd or was accepted so readily and with such an absence of criticism. It so suited the people of the upper classes that to this day, notwithstanding its entirely fantastic character and the arbitrary nature of its assertions, it is repeated by learned and unlearned as though it were something indubitable and self-evident.

Habent sua fata libelli pro capite lectoris,[4] and so, or even more so, theories *habent sua fata* according to the condition of error in which that society is living among whom and for whom the theories are invented. If a theory justifies the

4 [This quotation, line 255 from *De litteris, syllabis, et metris* (c. 240 A.D.) by Terentianus Maurus, correctly reads *Pro captu lectoris habent sua fata libelli,* "The fate of books depends upon the head (understanding) of the reader."—ED.]

false position in which a certain part of a society is living, then, however unfounded or even obviously false the theory may be, it is accepted and becomes an article of faith to that section of society. Such, for instance, was the celebrated and unfounded theory, expounded by Malthus, of the tendency of the population of the world to increase in geometrical progression but of the means of sustenance to increase only in arithmetical progression, and of the consequent overpopulation of the world; such, also, was the theory (an outgrowth of the Malthusian) of selection and struggle for existence as the basis of human progress. Such, again, is Marx's theory, which regards the gradual destruction of small private production by large capitalistic production, now going on around us, as an inevitable decree of fate. However unfounded such theories are, however contrary to all that is known and confessed by humanity, and however obviously immoral they may be, they are accepted with credulity, pass uncriticized, and are preached, perchance for centuries, until the conditions are destroyed which they served to justify or until their absurdity has become too evident. To this class belongs this astonishing theory of the Baumgartenian trinity—goodness, beauty, and truth—according to which it appears that the very best that can be done by the art of nations after 1900 years of Christian teaching is to choose as the ideal of their life the ideal that was held by a small, semi-savage, slaveholding people who lived 2000 years ago, who imitated the nude human body extremely well, and erected buildings pleasant to look at. All these incompatibilities pass completely unnoticed. Learned people write long, cloudy treatises on beauty as a member of the aesthetic trinity of beauty, truth, and goodness: *das Schöne, das Wahre, das Gute; le Beau, le Vrai, le Bon,* are repeated with capital letters by philosophers, aestheticians, and artists, by private individuals, by novelists, and by feuilletonistes, and they all think, when pronouncing these sacrosanct words, that they speak of something quite definite and solid—something on which they can base their opinions. In reality, these words not only have no definite meaning, but they hinder us in attaching any definite meaning to existing art; they are wanted only for the purpose of justifying the false importance we attribute to an art that transmits every kind of feeling, if only those feelings afford us pleasure.

CHAPTER EIGHT

BUT if art is a human activity having for its purpose the transmission to others of the highest and best feelings to which men have risen, how could it be that humanity for a certain rather considerable period of its existence (from the time people ceased to believe in Church doctrine down to the present day) should exist without this important activity, and, instead of it, should put up with an insignificant artistic activity only affording pleasure?

In order to answer this question it is necessary, first of all, to correct the current error people make in attributing to our art the significance of true, universal art. We are so accustomed, not only naïvely to consider the Circassian family the best stock of people, but also the Anglo-Saxon race the best race if we are Englishmen or Americans, or the Teutonic if we are Germans, or the Gallo-Latin if we are French, or the Slavonic if we are Russians, that, when speaking of our own art, we feel fully convinced, not only that our art is true art, but even that it is the best and only true art. But in reality our art is not only not the only art (as the Bible once was held to be the only book), but it is not even the art of the whole of Christendom—only of a small section of that part of humanity. It was correct to speak of a national Jewish, Grecian, or Egyptian art, and one may speak of a now-existing Chinese, Japanese, or Indian art shared in by a whole people. Such art, common to a whole nation, existed in Russia till Peter the First's time, and existed in the rest of Europe until the thirteenth or fourteenth century; but since the upper classes of European society, having lost faith in the Church teaching, did not accept real Christianity but remained without any faith, one can no longer speak of an art of the Christian nations in the sense of the whole of art. Since the upper classes of the Christian nations lost faith in Church Christianity, the art of those upper classes has separated itself from the art of the rest of the people, and there have been two arts—the art of the people and genteel art. And therefore the answer to the question, How could it occur that humanity lived for a certain period without real art, replacing it by art which served enjoyment only?, is that not all humanity, nor even any considerable portion of it, lived without real art, but only the highest classes of European Christian society, and even they only for a comparatively short time—from the beginning of the Renaissance down to our own day.

And the consequence of this absence of true art showed itself, inevitably, in the corruption of that class which nourished itself on the false art. All the confused, unintelligible theories of art, all the false and contradictory judgments on art, and particularly the self-confident stagnation of our art in its false path, all arise from the assertion which has come into common use and is accepted as an unquestioned truth, but is yet amazingly and palpably false—the assertion, namely, that the art of our upper classes [1] is the whole of art, the true, the only, the universal art. And although this assertion (which is precisely similar to the assertion made by religious people of the various Churches who consider that theirs is the only true religion) is quite arbitrary and obviously unjust, yet it is calmly repeated by all the people of our circle with full faith in its infallibility.

The art we have is the whole of art, the real, the only art, and yet two-thirds of the human race (all the peoples of Asia and Africa) live and die knowing nothing of this sole and supreme art. And even in our Christian society hardly one per cent of the people make use of this art which we speak of

[1] The contrast made is between the classes and the masses, between those who do not and those who do earn their bread by productive manual labor, the middle classes being taken as an offshoot of the upper classes.—TR.

as being the *whole* of art; the remaining ninety-nine per cent live and die, generation after generation, crushed by toil, and never tasting this art which, moreover, is of such a nature that, if they could get it, they would not understand anything of it. We, according to the current aesthetic theory, acknowledge art as one of the highest manifestations of the Idea, God, Beauty, or as the highest spiritual enjoyment; furthermore, we hold that all people have equal rights, if not to material, at any rate to spiritual well-being; and yet ninety-nine per cent of our European population live and die, generation after generation, crushed by toil, much of which toil is necessary for the production of our art which they never use, and we, nevertheless, calmly assert that the art which we produce is the real, true, only art—all of art!

To the remark that if our art is the true art everyone should have the benefit of it, the usual reply is that if not everybody at present makes use of existing art the fault lies not in the art but in the false organization of society; that one can imagine to oneself, in the future, a state of things in which physical labor will be partly superseded by machinery, partly lightened by its just distribution, and that labor for the production of art will be taken in turns; that there is no need for some people always to sit below the stage moving the decorations, winding up the machinery, working at the piano or French horn, and setting type and printing books, but that the people who do all this work might be engaged only a few hours per day, and in their leisure time might enjoy all the blessings of art.

That is what the defenders of our exclusive art say. But I think they do not themselves believe it. They cannot help knowing that fine art can arise only on the slavery of the masses of the people, and can continue only as long as that slavery lasts, and they cannot help knowing that only under conditions of intense labor for the workers can specialists—writers, musicians, dancers, and actors—arrive at that fine degree of perfection to which they do attain, or produce their refined works of art; and only under the same conditions can there be a fine public to esteem such productions. Free the slaves of capital, and it will be impossible to produce such refined art.

But even were we to admit the inadmissible and say that means may be found by which art (that art which among us is considered to be art) may be accessible to the whole people, another consideration presents itself showing that fashionable art cannot be the whole of art, viz., the fact that it is completely unintelligible to the people. Formerly men wrote poems in Latin, but now their artistic productions are as unintelligible to the common folk as if they were written in Sanscrit. The usual reply to this is that if the people do not now understand this art of ours it only proves that they are undeveloped, and that this has been so at each fresh step forward made by art. First it was not understood, but afterward people got accustomed to it.

"It will be the same with our present art; it will be understood when everybody is as well educated as we are—the people of the upper classes—who produce this art," say the defenders of our art. But this assertion is evidently even more unjust than the former, for we know that the majority of the productions of the art of the upper classes, such as various odes, poems, dramas, cantatas, pastorals, pictures, etc., which delighted the people of the upper classes when they were produced, never were afterward either understood or valued by the great masses of mankind, but have remained what they were at first—a mere pastime for rich people of their time, for whom alone they ever were of any importance. It is also often urged, in proof of the assertion that the people will some day understand our art, that some productions of so-called "classical" poetry, music, or painting, which formerly did not please the masses, do—now that they have been offered to them from all sides—begin to please these same masses; but this only shows that the crowd, especially the half-spoiled town crowd, can easily (its taste having been perverted) be accustomed to any sort of art. Moreover, this art is not produced by these masses, nor even chosen by them, but is energetically thrust upon them in those public places in which art is accessible to the people. For the great majority of working-people, our art, besides being inaccessible on account of its costliness, is strange in its very nature, transmitting as it does the feelings of people far removed from those conditions of laborious life which are natural to the great body of humanity. That which is enjoyment to a man of the rich classes is incomprehensible as a pleasure to a workingman, and evokes in him either no feeling at all or only a feeling quite contrary to that which it evokes in an idle and satiated man. Such feelings as form the chief subjects of present-day art—say, for instance, honor,[2] patriotism, and amorousness—evoke in a workingman only bewilderment and contempt, or indignation. So that even if a possibility were given to the laboring classes in their free time to see, to read, and to hear all that forms the flower of contemporary art (as is done to some extent in towns by means of picture galleries, popular concerts, and libraries), the workingman (to the extent to which he is a laborer and has not begun to pass into the ranks of those perverted by idleness) would be able to make nothing of our fine art, and if he did understand it, that which he understood would not elevate his soul but would certainly, in most cases, pervert it. To thoughtful and sincere people there can, therefore, be no doubt that the art of our upper classes never can be the art of the whole people. But if art is an important matter, a spiritual blessing, essential for all men ("like religion," as the devotees of art are fond of saying), then it should be accessible to everyone. And if, as in our day, it is not accessible to all men, then one of two things: either art is not the vital matter it is represented to be or that art which we call art is not the real thing.

The dilemma is inevitable and therefore clever and immoral people avoid it by denying one side of it, viz., denying that the common people have a right to art. These people simply and boldly speak out (what lies at the heart of the matter), and say that the participators in and utilizers of what, in

2 Dueling was still customary among the higher circles in Russia, as in other continental countries.—TR.

their esteem, is highly beautiful art, i.e., art furnishing the greatest enjoyment, can only be "schöne Geister," "the elect," [3] as the romanticists called them, the "Übermenschen," [4] as they are called by the followers of Nietzsche; the remaining vulgar herd, incapable of experiencing these pleasures, must serve the exalted pleasures of this superior breed of people. The people who express these views at least do not pretend and do not try to combine the incombinable, but frankly admit what is the case—that our art is an art of the upper classes only. So essentially art has been, and is, understood by everyone engaged in it in our society.

CHAPTER NINE

THE unbelief of the upper classes of the European world had this effect—that instead of an artistic activity aiming at transmitting the highest feelings to which humanity has attained, those flowing from religious perception, we have an activity which aims at affording the greatest enjoyment to a certain class of society. And of all the immense domain of art, that part has been fenced off and is alone called art which affords enjoyment to the people of this particular circle.

Apart from the moral effects on European society of such a selection from the whole sphere of art of what did not deserve such a valuation, and the acknowledgment of it as important art, this perversion of art has weakened art itself and well-nigh destroyed it. The first great result was that art was deprived of the infinite, varied, and profound religious subject matter proper to it. The second result was that having only a small circle of people in view, it lost its beauty of form and became affected and obscure; and the third and chief

[3] [A more correct rendering of "schöne Geister" would be "men who are able to perceive the beautiful."—ED.]

[4] [It seems to be arbitrary to identify the Romantic concept of "schöne Geister" with Nietzsche's concept of the "Übermensch."—ED.]

result was that it ceased to be either natural or even sincere and became thoroughly artifical and brain-spun.

The first result—the impoverishment of subject matter—followed because only that is a true work of art which transmits fresh feelings not before experienced by man. As a thought product is only then a real thought product when it transmits new conceptions and thoughts and does not merely repeat what was known before, so also an art product is only then a genuine art product when it brings a new feeling (however insignificant) into the current of human life. This explains why children and youths are so strongly impressed by those works of art which first transmit to them feelings they had not before experienced.

The same powerful impression is made on people by feelings which are quite new and have never before been expressed by man. And it is the source from which such feelings flow of which the art of the upper classes has deprived itself by estimating feelings, not in conformity with religious perception, but according to the degree of enjoyment they afford. There is nothing older and more hackneyed than enjoyment, and there is nothing fresher than the feelings springing from the religious consciousness of each age. It could not be otherwise: man's enjoyment has limits established by his nature, but the movement forward of humanity, that which is voiced by religious perception, has no limits. At every forward step taken by humanity—and such steps are taken in consequence of the greater and greater elucidation of religious perception—men experience new and fresh feelings. And therefore only on the basis of religious perception (which shows the highest level of life-comprehension reached by the men of a certain period) can fresh emotion, never before felt by man, arise. From the religious perception of the ancient Greeks flowed the really new, important, and endlessly varied feelings expressed by Homer and the tragic writers. It was the same among the Jews, who attained the religious conception of a single God—from that perception flowed all those new and important emotions expressed by the prophets. It was the same for the poets of the Middle Ages who, if they believed in a heavenly hierarchy, believed also in the Catholic commune; and it is the same for a man of today who has grasped the religious conception of true Christianity, the brotherhood of man.

The variety of fresh feelings flowing from religious perception is endless, and they are all new; for religious perception is nothing else than the first indication of that which is coming into existence, viz., the new relation of man to the world around him. But the feelings flowing from the desire for enjoyment are, on the contrary, not only limited, but were long ago experienced and expressed. And therefore the lack of belief of the upper classes of Europe has left them with an art fed on the poorest subject matter.

The impoverishment of the subject matter of upper-class art was further increased by the fact that, ceasing to be religious, it ceased also to be popular, and this again diminished the range of feelings which it transmitted. For the range of feelings experienced by the powerful and the rich who have no experience of labor for the support of life is far poorer, more limited, and more insignificant than the range of feelings natural to working-people.

People of our circle, aestheticians, usually think and say just the contrary of this. I remember how Gontchareff, the author, a very clever and educated man but a thorough townsman and an aesthetician, said to me that after Turgenev's *Memoirs of a Sportsman* there was nothing left to write about in peasant life. It was all used up. The life of working people seemed to him so simple that Turgenev's peasant stories had used up all there was to describe. The life of our wealthy people, with their love affairs and dissatisfaction with themselves, seemed to him full of inexhaustible subject matter. One hero kissed his lady on her palm, another on her elbow, and a third somewhere else. One man is discontented through idleness, and another because people don't love him. And Gontchareff thought that in this sphere there is no end of variety. And this opinion—that the life of working people is

poor in subject matter, but that our life, the life of the idle, is
full of interest—is shared by very many people in our society.
The life of a laboring man, with its endlessly varied forms of
labor and the dangers connected with this labor on sea and
underground; his migrations, the intercourse with his em-
ployers, overseers, and companions, and with men of other
religions and other nationalities; his struggles with nature
and with wild beasts, the associations with domestic animals,
the work in the forest, on the steppe, in the field, the garden,
the orchard; his intercourse with wife and children, not only
as with people near and dear to him, but as with co-workers
and helpers in labor, replacing him in time of need; his concern in all economic questions, not as matters of display or
discussion, but as problems of life for himself and his family;
his pride in self-suppression and service to others, his pleasures of refreshment; and with all these interests permeated by
a religious attitude toward these occurrences—all this to us
who have not these interests and possess no religious perception seems monotonous in comparison with those small en-
joyments and insignificant cares of our life—a life not of labor
nor of production, but of consumption and destruction of
that which others have produced for us. We think the feelings experienced by people of our day and our class are very
important and varied; but in reality almost all the feelings
of people of our class amount to but three very insignificant
and simple feelings—the feeling of pride, the feeling of sexual
desire, and the feeling of weariness of life. These three feelings, with their outgrowths, form almost the only subject matter of the art of the rich classes.

At first, at the very beginning of the separation of the exclusive art of the upper classes from universal art, its chief
subject matter was the feeling of pride. It was so at the time
of the Renaissance and after it, when the chief subject of
works of art was the laudation of the strong—popes, kings,
and dukes; odes and madrigals were written in their honor,
and they were extolled in cantatas and hymns; their portraits
were painted and their statues carved, in various adulatory

ways. Next, the element of sexual desire began more and more to enter into art, and (with very few exceptions, and in novels and dramas almost without exception) it has now become an essential feature of every art product of the rich classes.

The third feeling transmitted by the art of the rich—that of discontent with life—appeared yet later in modern art. This feeling, which at the beginning of the present century was expressed only by exceptional men, by Byron, by Leopardi, and afterward by Heine, has latterly become fashionable and is expressed by most ordinary and empty people. Most justly does the French critic Doumic characterize the works of the new writers:

> C'est la lassitude de vivre, le mépris de l'époque présente, le regret d'un autre temps aperçu à travers l'illusion de l'art, le goût du paradoxe, le besoin de se singulariser, une aspiration de raffinés vers la simplicité, l'adoration enfantine du merveilleux, la séduction maladive de la rêverie, l'ébranlement des nerfs—surtout l'appel exaspéré de la sensualité (*Les Jeunes, René Doumic*).[1]

And, as a matter of fact, of these three feelings it is sensuality, the lowest (accessible not only to all men, but even to all animals), which forms the chief subject matter of works of art of recent times.

From Boccaccio to Marcel Prévost, all the novels, poems, and verses invariably transmit the feeling of sexual love in its different forms. Adultery is not only the favorite, but almost the only theme of all the novels. A performance is not a performance unless, under some pretense, women appear with naked busts and limbs. Songs and romances—all are expressions of lust idealized in various degrees.

A majority of the pictures by French artists represent female nakedness in various forms. In recent French literature

[1] [It is weariness of life, contempt for the present epoch, regret for another time seen through the illusion of art, the taste for paradox, the necessity to set one's self apart, a hyper-sensitive aspiration toward simplicity, a childish adoration of the marvelous, the sick seduction of dreams, the shattering of the nerves—and especially the exasperated demands of sensuality.—ED.]

there is hardly a page or poem in which nakedness is not described, and in which, relevantly or irrelevantly, their favorite thought and word, *nu,* is not repeated a couple of times. There is a certain writer, René de Gourmond, who gets printed and is considered talented. To get an idea of the new writers, I read his novel, *Les Chevaux de Diomède.* It is a consecutive and detailed account of the sexual connections some gentleman had with various women. Every page contains lust-kindling descriptions. It is the same in Pierre Louys' book, *Aphrodite,* which met with success; it is the same in a book I lately chanced upon, Huysmans' *Certains,* and, with but few exceptions, it is the same in all the French novels. They are all the productions of people suffering from erotic mania. And these people are evidently convinced that as their whole life, in consequence of their diseased condition, is concentrated on amplifying various sexual abominations, therefore the life of all the world is similarly concentrated. And these people, suffering from erotic mania, are imitated throughout the whole artistic world of Europe and America.

Thus in consequence of the lack of belief and the exceptional manner of life of the wealthy classes, the art of those classes became impoverished in its subject matter, and has sunk to the transmission of the feelings of pride, discontent with life, and, above all, of sexual desire.

CHAPTER TEN

IN consequence of their unbelief, the art of the upper classes became poor in subject matter. But besides that, becoming continually more and more exclusive, it became at the same time continually more and more involved, affected, and obscure.

When a universal artist (such as were some of the Grecian artists or the Jewish prophets) composed his work, he naturally strove to say what he had to say in such a manner that his production should be intelligible to all men. But when an artist composed for a small circle of people placed in exceptional conditions, or even for a single individual and his courtiers—for popes, cardinals, kings, dukes, queens, or for a king's mistress—he naturally only aimed at influencing these people, who were well known to him and lived in exceptional conditions familiar to him. And this was an easier task, and the artist was involuntarily drawn to express himself by allusions comprehensible only to the initiated, and obscure to everyone else. In the first place, more could be said in this way; and secondly, there is (for the initiated) even a certain charm in the cloudiness of such a manner of expression. This method, which showed itself both in euphemism and in mythological and historical allusions, came more and more into use until it has, apparently, at last reached its utmost limits in the so-called art of the Decadents. It has come, finally, to this: that not only is haziness, mysteriousness, obscurity, and exclusiveness (shutting out the masses) elevated to the rank of a merit and a condition of poetic art, but even incorrectness, indefiniteness, and lack of eloquence are held in esteem.

Théophile Gautier, in his preface to the celebrated *Fleurs du Mal,* says that Baudelaire, as far as possible, banished from poetry eloquence, passion, and truth too strictly copied (*"l'éloquence, la passion, et la vérité calquée trop exactement"*).

And Baudelaire not only expressed this, but maintained his thesis in his verses and, yet more strikingly, in the prose of his *Petits Poèmes en Prose,* the meanings of which have to be guessed like a rebus, and remain for the most part undiscovered.

The poet Verlaine (who followed next after Baudelaire and was also esteemed great) even wrote an "Art Poétique," in which he advises this style of composition:

> De la musique avant toute chose,
> Et pour cela préfère l'Impair

Plus vague et plus soluble dans l'air,
Sans rien en lui qui pèse ou qui pose.

Il faut aussi que tu n'ailles point
Choisir tes mots sans quelque méprise:
Rien de plus cher que la chanson grise
Où l'Indécis au Précis se joint.

*   *   *   *   *

And again:

De la musique encore et toujours!
Que ton vers soit la chose envolée
Qu'on sent qui fuit d'une âme en allée
Vers d'autres cieux à d'autres amours.

Que ton vers soit la bonne aventure
Eparse au vent crispé du matin,
Qui va fleurant la menthe et le thym . . . .
Et tout le reste est littérature.[1]

After these two comes Mallarmé, considered the most important of the young poets, and he plainly says that the charm of poetry lies in our having to guess its meaning—that in poetry there should always be a puzzle:

[1] Music, music before all things
The eccentric still prefer,
Vague in air, and nothing weighty,
Soluble. Yet do not err,

Choosing words; still do it lightly,
Do it too with some contempt;
Dearest is the song that's tipsy,
Clearness, dimness not exempt.

———————————

Music always, now and ever
Be thy verse the thing that flies
From a soul that's gone, escaping,
Gone to other loves and skies.

Gone to other loves and regions,
Following fortunes that allure,
Mint and thyme and morning crispness . . . .
All the rest's mere literature.

Je pense qu'il faut qu'il n'y ait qu'allusion (says he). *La contemplation des objets, l'image s'envolant des rêveries suscitées par eux, sont le chant: les Parnassiens, eux, prennent la chose entièrement et la montrent; par là ils manquent de mystère; ils retirent aux esprits cette joie délicieuse de croire qu'ils créent.* Nommer un objet, c'est supprimer les trois quarts de la jouissance du poème, qui est faite du bonheur de deviner peu à peu: le suggérer, voilà le rêve. *C'est le parfait usage de ce mystère qui constitue le symbole: évoquer petit à petit un objet pour montrer un état d'âme, ou, inversement, choisir un objet et en dégager un état d'âme, par une série de déchiffrements.*
     ... Si un être d'une intelligence moyenne, et d'une préparation littéraire insuffisante, ouvre par hasard un livre ainsi fait et prétend en jouir, il y a un malentendu, il faut remettre les choses à leur place. Il doit y avoir toujours énigme en poésie, *et c'est le but de la littérature, il n'y en a pas d'autre, —d'évoquer les objets.*[2]—Enquête sur l'Évolution Littéraire,
                                                    Jules Huret, pp. 60, 61.

Thus is obscurity elevated into a dogma among the new poets. As the French critic Doumic (who has not yet accepted the dogma) quite correctly says:

     Il serait temps aussi d'en finir avec cette fameuse "théorie de l'obscurite" que la nouvelle école a élevée, en effet, à la hauteur d'un dogme.—*Les Jeunes,* par René Doumic.[3]

[2] I think there should be nothing but allusions. The contemplation of objects, the fleeing image of reveries evoked by them, are the song. The Parnassiens state the thing completely, and show it, and thereby lack mystery; they deprive the mind of that delicious joy of imagining that it creates. To *name an object is to take three-quarters of the enjoyment of the poem, which consists in the happiness of guessing little by little: to suggest, that is the dream.* It is the perfect use of this mystery that constitutes the symbol: little by little, to evoke an object in order to show a state of the soul; or, inversely, to choose an object, and from it to disengage a state of the soul by a series of decipherings.
     . . . If a being of mediocre intelligence and insufficient literary preparation chance to open a book made in this way and pretends to enjoy it, there is a misunderstanding—things must be returned to their places. *There should always be an enigma in poetry,* and the aim of literature— it has no other—is to evoke objects.
[3] It were time also to have done with this famous "theory of obscurity," which the new school has, in effect, raised to the height of a dogma.

But it is not French writers only who think thus. The poets of all other countries think and act in the same way: German, and Scandinavian, and Italian, and Russian, and English. So also do the artists of the new period in all branches of art: in painting, in sculpture, and in music. Relying on Nietzsche and Wagner, the artists of the new age conclude that it is unnecessary for them to be intelligible to the vulgar crowd; it is enough for them to evoke poetic emotion in "the finest nurtured," to borrow a phrase from an English aesthetician.

In order that what I am saying may not seem to be mere assertion, I will quote at least a few examples from the French poets who have led this movement. The name of these poets is legion. I have taken French writers, because they, more decidedly than any others, indicate the new direction of art and are imitated by most European writers.

Besides those whose names are already considered famous, such as Baudelaire and Verlaine, here are the names of a few of them: Jean Moréas, Charles Morice, Henri de Régnier, Charles Vignier, Adrien Remacle, René Ghil, Maurice Maeterlinck, G. Albert Aurier, Rémy de Gourmont, Saint-Pol-Roux-le-Magnifique, Georges Rodenbach, le comte Robert de Montesquiou-Fezensac. These are Symbolists and Decadents. Next we have the "Magi": Joséphin Péladan, Paul Adam, Jules Bois, M. Papus, and others.

Besides these, there are yet one hundred and forty-one others whom Doumic mentions in the book referred to above.

Here are some examples from the work of those of them who are considered to be the best, beginning with that most celebrated man, acknowledged to be a great artist worthy of a monument—Baudelaire. This is a poem from his celebrated *Fleurs du Mal:*

No. XXIV

Je t'adore à l'égal de la voûte nocturne,
O vase de tristesse, ô grande taciturne,
Et t'aime d'autant plus, belle, que tu me fuis,

Et que tu me parais, ornement de mes nuits,
Plus ironiquement accumuler les lieues
Qui séparent mes bras des immensités bleues.

Je m'avance à l'attaque, et je grimpe aux assauts,
Comme après un cadavre un choeur de vermisseaux,
Et je chéris, ô bête implacable et cruelle,
Jusqu'à cette froideur par où tu m'es plus belle! [4]

And this is another by the same writer:

No. XXXVI

DUELLUM

Deux guerriers ont couru l'un sur l'autre; leurs armes
Ont éclaboussé l'air de lueurs et de sang.
Ces jeux, ces cliquetis du fer sont les vacarmes
D'une jeunesse en proie à l'amour vagissant.

Les glaives sont brisés! comme notre jeunesse,
Ma chère! Mais les dents, les ongles acérés,
Vengent bientôt l'épée et la dague traîtresse.
O fureur des coeurs mûrs par l'amour ulcérés!

Dans le ravin hanté des chats-pards et des onces
Nos héros, s'étreignant méchamment, ont roulé,
Et leur peau fleurira l'aridité des ronces.

Ce gouffre, c'est l'enfer, de nos amis peuplé!
Roulons-y sans remords, amazone inhumaine,
Afin d'éterniser l'ardeur de notre haine! [5]

To be exact, I should mention that the collection contains verses less comprehensible than these but not one poem which is plain and can be understood without a certain effort—an effort seldom rewarded, for the feelings which the poet transmits are evil and very low ones. And these feelings are always, and purposely, expressed by him with eccentricity and lack of clearness. This premeditated obscurity is especially notice-

[4] For translation, see Appendix I.
[5] For translation, see Appendix I.

able in his prose where the author could, if he liked, speak plainly.

Take, for instance, the first piece from his *Petits Poèmes:*

"L'ETRANGER"

Qui aimes-tu le mieux, homme énigmatique, dis? ton père, ta mère, ta soeur, ou ton frère?

Je n'ai ni père, ni mère, ni soeur, ni frère.

Tes amis?

Vous vous servez là d'une parole dont le sens m'est resté jusqu'à ce jour inconnu.

Ta patrie?

J'ignore sous quelle latitude elle est située.

La beauté?

Je l'aimerais volontiers, déesse et immortelle.

L'or?

Je le hais comme vous haïssez Dieu.

Et qu'aimes-tu donc, extraordinaire étranger?

J'aime les nuages . . . . les nuages qui passent . . . . là-bas,
. . . . les merveilleux nuages! [6]

The piece called "La Soupe et les Nuages" is probably intended to express the unintelligibility of the poet even to her whom he loves. This is the piece in question:

Ma petite folle bien-aimée me donnait à dîner, et par la fenêtre ouverte de la salle à manger je contemplais les mouvantes architectures que Dieu fait avec les vapeurs, les merveilleuses constructions de l'impalpable. Et je me disais, à travers ma contemplation: "Toutes ces fantasmagories sont presque aussi belles que les yeux de ma belle bien-aimée, la petite folle monstrueuse aux yeux verts."

Et tout à coup je reçus un violent coup de poing dans le dos, et j'entendis une voix rauque et charmante, une voix hystérique et comme enrouée par l'eau-de-vie, la voix de ma chère petite bien-aimée, qui me disait, "Allez-vous bientôt manger votre soupe, s . . . . b . . . . de marchand de nuages?" [7]

[6] For translation, see Appendix I.
[7] For translation, see Appendix I.

However artificial these two pieces may be, it is still possible, with some effort, to guess at what the author meant them to express, but some of the pieces are absolutely incomprehensible—at least to me. "Le Galant Tireur" is a piece I was quite unable to understand.

LE GALANT TIREUR

Comme la voiture traversait le bois, il la fit arrêter dans le voisinage d'un tir, disant qu'il lui serait agréable de tirer quelques balles pour tuer le Temps. Tuer ce monstre-là n'est-ce pas l'occupation la plus ordinaire et la plus légitime de chacun?—Et il offrit galamment la main à sa chère, délicieuse et exécrable femme, à cette mystérieuse femme à laquelle il doit tant de plaisirs, tant de douleurs, et peut-être aussi une grande partie de son génie.

Plusieurs balles frappèrent loin du but proposé; l'une d'elles s'enfonça même dans le plafond; et comme la charmante créature riait follement, se moquant de la maladresse de son époux, celui-ci se tourna brusquement vers elle, et lui dit: "Observez cette poupée, là-bas, à droite, qui porte le nez en l'air et qui a la mine si hautaine. Eh bien! cher ange, je me figure que c'est vous." Et il ferma les yeux et il lâcha la détente. La poupée fut nettement décapitée.

Alors s'inclinant vers sa chère, sa délicieuse, son exécrable femme, son inévitable et impitoyable Muse, et lui baisant respectueusement la main, il ajouta: "Ah! mon cher ange, combien je vous remercie de mon adresse! [8]

The productions of another celebrity, Verlaine, are not less affected and unintelligible. This, for instance, is the first poem in the section called "Ariettes Oubliées."

> *"Le vent dans la plaine*
> *Suspend son haleine."*
> —FAVART.

C'est l'extase langoureuse,
C'est la fatigue amoureuse,
C'est tous les frissons des bois

---

[8] For translation, see Appendix I.

Parmi l'étreinte des brises,
C'est, vers les ramures grises,
Le choeur des petites voix.

O le frêle et frais murmure!
Cela gazouille et susurre,
Cela ressemble au cri doux
Que l'herbe agitée expire . . . .
Tu dirais, sous l'eau qui vire,
Le roulis sourd des cailloux.

Cette âme qui se lamente
En cette plainte dormante
C'est la nôtre, n'est-ce pas?
La mienne, dis, et la tienne,
Dont s'exhale l'humble antienne
Par ce tiède soir, tout bas? [9]

What "choeur des petites voix," and what "cri doux que l'herbe agitée expire," and what it all means, remains altogether unintelligible to me.

And here is another "Ariette":

VIII

Dans l'interminable
Ennui de la plaine,
La neige incertaine
Luit comme du sable.

Le ciel est de cuivre,
Sans lueur aucune.
On croirait voir vivre
Et mourir la lune.

Comme des nuées
Flottent gris les chênes
Des forêts prochaines
Parmi les buées.

[9] For translation, see Appendix I.

Le ciel est de cuivre,
Sans lueur aucune.
On croirait voir vivre
Et mourir la lune.

Corneille poussive
Et vous, les loups maigres,
Par ces bises aigres
Quoi donc vous arrive?

Dans l'interminable
Ennui de la plaine,
La neige incertaine
Luit comme du sable.[10]

How does the moon seem to live and die in a copper heaven? And how can snow shine like sand? The whole thing is not merely unintelligible, but, under pretense of conveying an impression, it passes off a string of incorrect comparisons and words.

Besides these artificial and obscure poems there are others which are intelligible, but which make up for it by being altogether bad, both in form and in subject. Such are all the poems under the heading "La Sagesse." The chief place in these verses is occupied by a very poor expression of the most commonplace Roman Catholic and patriotic sentiments. For instance, one meets with verses such as this:

Je ne veux plus penser qu'à ma mère Marie,
Siège de la sagesse et source de pardons,
Mère de France aussi *de qui nous attendons*
Inébranlablement l'honneur de la patrie.[11]

Before citing examples from other poets I must pause to note the amazing celebrity of these two versifiers, Baudelaire

10 For translation, see Appendix I.
11 I do not wish to think any more, except about my mother Mary,
   Seat of wisdom and source of pardon,
   Also Mother of France, *from whom we*
   Steadfastly expect the honor of our country.

and Verlaine, who are now accepted as being great poets. How the French, who had Chénier, Musset, Lamartine, and, above all, Hugo—and among whom quite recently flourished the so-called Parnassiens: Leconte de Lisle, Sully-Prudhomme, etc.—could attribute such importance to these two versifiers, who were far from skillful in form and most contemptible and commonplace in subject matter, is to me incomprehensible. The conception of life of one of them, Baudelaire, consisted in elevating gross egotism into a theory, and replacing morality by a cloudy conception of beauty and especially artificial beauty. Baudelaire had a preference, which he expressed, for a woman's face painted rather than showing its natural color, and for metal trees and a theatrical imitation of water rather than real trees and real water.

The life-conception of the other, Verlaine, consisted in weak profligacy, confession of his moral impotence, and, as an antidote to that impotence, in the grossest Roman Catholic idolatry. Both, moreover, were quite lacking in naïveté, sincerity, and simplicity, and both overflowed with artificiality, forced originality and self-assurance. So that in their least bad productions one sees more of M. Baudelaire or M. Verlaine than of what they were describing. But these two indifferent versifiers form a school and lead hundreds of followers after them.

There is only one explanation of this fact: it is that the art of the society in which these versifiers lived is not a serious, important matter of life, but is a mere amusement. And all amusements grow wearisome by repetition. And, in order to make wearisome amusement again tolerable, it is necessary to find some means to freshen it up. When, at cards, ombre grows stale, whist is introduced; when whist grows stale, écarté is substituted; when écarté grows stale, some other novelty is invented, and so on. The substance of the matter remains the same, only its form is changed. And so it is with this kind of art. The subject matter of the art of the upper classes growing continually more and more limited, it has come at last to this, that to the artists of these exclusive classes it seems as if everything has already been said and that to find anything new to say is impossible. And therefore, to freshen up this art they look out for fresh forms.

Baudelaire and Verlaine invent such a new form, furbish it up, moreover, with hitherto unused pornographic details, and—the critics and the public of the upper classes hail them as great writers.

This is the only explanation of the success, not of Baudelaire and Verlaine only, but of all the Decadents.

For instance, there are poems by Mallarmé and Maeterlinck which have no meaning, and yet for all that, or perhaps on that very account, are printed by tens of thousands, not only in various publications but even in collections of the best works of the younger poets.

This, for example, is a sonnet by Mallarmé:

A la nue accablante tu
Basse de basalte et de laves
A même les échos esclaves
Par une troupe sans vertu.

Quel sépulcral naufrage (tu
Le soir, écume, mais y baves)
Suprême une entre les épaves
Abolit le mât dévêtu.

Ou cela que furibond faute
De quelque perdition haute
Tout l'abîme vain éployé
Dans le si blanc cheveu qui traîne
Avarement aura noyé
Le flanc enfant d'une sirène.[12]

(*Pan,* 1895, No. i.)

This poem is not exceptional in its incomprehensibility. I have read several poems by Mallarmé, and they also had no meaning whatever. I give a sample of his prose in Appendix I.

[12] This sonnet seems too unintelligible for translation.—Tr.

There is a whole volume of this prose called *Divagations*. It is impossible to understand any of it. And that is evidently what the author intended.

And here is a song by Maeterlinck, another celebrated author of today:

Quand il est sorti,
(J'entendis la porte)
Quand il est sorti
Elle avait souri . . . .

Mais quand il entra
(J'entendis la lampe)
Mais quand il entra
Une autre était là . . . .

Et j'ai vu la mort,
(J'entendis son âme)
Et j'ai vu la mort
Qui l'attend encore . . . .

On est venu dire,
(Mon enfant j'ai peur)
On est venu dire
Qu'il allait partir . . . .

Ma lampe allumée,
(Mon enfant j'ai peur)
Ma lampe allumée
Me suis approchée . . . .

A la première porte,
(Mon enfant j'ai peur)
A la première porte,
La flamme a tremblé . . . .

A la seconde porte,
(Mon enfant j'ai peur)
A la seconde porte,
La flamme a parlé . . . .

A la troisième porte,
(Mon enfant j'ai peur)
A la troisième porte,
La lumière est morte . . . .

Et s'il revenait un jour
Que faut-il lui dire?
Dites-lui qu'on l'attendit
Jusqu'à s'en mourir . . . .

Et s'il demande où vous êtes
Que faut-il répondre?
Donnez-lui mon anneau d'or
Sans rien lui répondre . . . .

Et s'il m'interroge alors
Sur la dernière heure?
Dites lui que j'ai souri
De peur qu'il ne pleure . . . .

Et s'il m'interroge encore
Sans me reconnaître?
Parlez-lui comme une soeur,
Il souffre peut-être . . . .

Et s'il veut savoir pourquoi
La salle est déserte?
Montrez lui la lampe éteinte
Et la porte ouverte . . . .[13]

(*Pan*, 1895, No. 2.)

Who went out? Who came in? Who is speaking? Who died?
I beg the reader to be at the pains of reading through the
samples I cite in Appendix II of the celebrated and esteemed
young poets—Griffin, Verhaeren, Moréas, and Montesquiou.
It is important to do so in order to form a clear conception
of the present position of art, and not to suppose, as many do,
that Decadentism is an accidental and transitory phenomenon.

[13] For translation, see Appendix I.

To avoid the reproach of having selected the worst verses, I have copied out of each volume the poem which happened to stand on page 28.

All the other productions of these poets are equally unintelligible or can only be understood with great difficulty, and then not fully. All the productions of those hundreds of poets, of whom I have named a few, are the same in kind. And among the Germans, Swedes, Norwegians, Italians, and us Russians, similar verses are printed. And such productions are printed and made up into book form, if not by the million, then by the hundred thousand (some of these works sell in tens of thousands). For typesetting, paging, printing, and binding these books, millions and millions of working days are spent—not less, I think, than went to build the great pyramid. And this is not all. The same is going on in all the other arts: millions and millions of working days are being spent on the production of equally incomprehensible works in painting, in music, and in the drama.

Painting not only does not lag behind poetry in this matter, but rather outstrips it. Here is an extract from the diary of an amateur of art,[14] written when visiting the Paris exhibitions in 1894:

> I was today at three exhibitions: the Symbolists', the Impressionists', and the Neo-Impressionists'. I looked at the pictures conscientiously and carefully, but again felt the same stupefaction and ultimate indignation. The first exhibition, that of Camille Pissarro, was comparatively the most comprehensible, though the pictures were out of drawing, had no subject, and the colorings were most improbable. The drawing was so indefinite that you were sometimes unable to make out which way an arm or a head was turned. The subject was generally *"effets"*—*Effet de brouillard, Effet du soir, Soleil couchant.* There were some pictures with figures, but without subjects.
> In the coloring, bright blue and bright green predominated. And each picture had its special color, with which

[14] [Tolstoy's eldest daughter, Tatiana, Mme. Sukhotin. See Tolstoy: *What is Art?* in "The World's Classics," p. 170.—Ed.]

the whole picture was, as it were, splashed. For instance, in "A Girl Guarding Geese," the special color is *vert de gris*, and dots of it were splashed about everywhere; on the face, the hair, the hands, and the clothes. In the same gallery— Durant Ruel—were other pictures by Puvis de Chavannes, Manet, Monet, Renoir, Sisley—who are all Impressionists. One of them, whose name I could not make out—it was something like Redon—had painted a blue face in profile. On the whole face there is only this blue tone, with white-of-lead. Pissarro has a water color all done in dots. In the foreground is a cow, entirely painted with varicolored dots. The general color cannot be distinguished, however much one stands back from, or draws near to, the picture. From there I went to see the Symbolists. I looked at them long without asking any one for an explanation, trying to guess the meaning; but it is beyond human comprehension. One of the first things to catch my eye was a wooden *haut-relief*, wretchedly executed, representing a woman (naked) who with both hands is squeezing from her two breasts streams of blood. The blood flows down, becoming lilac in color. Her hair first descends, and then rises again, and turns into trees. The figure is all colored yellow, and the hair is brown.

Next—a picture: a yellow sea, on which swims something which is neither a ship nor a heart; on the horizon is a profile with a halo and yellow hair, which changes into a sea, in which it is lost. Some of the painters lay on their colors so thickly that the effect is something between painting and sculpture. A third exhibit was even less comprehensible: a man's profile; before him a flame and black stripes—leeches, as I was afterwards told. At last I asked a gentleman who was there what it meant, and he explained to me that the *haut-relief* was a symbol, and that it represented *"La Terre."* The heart swimming in a yellow sea was *"Illusion perdue,"* and the gentleman with the leeches *"Le Mal."* There were also some Impressionist pictures: elementary profiles, holding some sort of flowers in their hands: in monotone, out of drawing, and either quite blurred or else marked out with wide black outlines.

This was in 1894; the same tendency is now even more strongly defined, and we have Böcklin, Stuck, Klinger, Sasha Schneider, and others.

The same thing is taking place in the drama. The play-

wrights give us an architect who, for some reason, has not fulfilled his former high intentions, and who consequently climbs
onto the roof of a house he has erected and tumbles down
head foremost; or an incomprehensible old woman (who ex-
terminates rats), and who, for an unintelligible reason, takes
a poetic child to the sea and there drowns him; or some blind
men who, sitting on the seashore, for some reason always repeat one and the same thing; or a bell of some kind which
flies into a lake and there rings.

And the same is happening in music—in that art which,
more than any other, one would have thought should be intelligible to everybody.

An acquaintance of yours, a musician of repute, sits down to
the piano and plays you what he says is a new composition of
his own, or of one of the new composers. You hear the strange,
loud sounds and admire the gymnastic exercises performed by
his fingers, and you see that the performer wishes to impress
upon you that the sounds he is producing express various
poetic strivings of the soul. You see his intention, but no feeling whatever is transmitted to you except weariness. The execution lasts long, or at least it seems very long to you because
you do not receive any clear impression, and involuntarily you
remember the words of Alphonse Karr, *"Plus ça va vite, plus
ça dure longtemps."* [15] And it occurs to you that perhaps it is
all a mystification; perhaps the performer is trying you—just
throwing his hands and fingers wildly about the keyboard in
the hope that you will fall into the trap and praise him, and
then he will laugh and confess that he only wanted to see if
he could hoax you. But when at last the piece does finish and
the perspiring and agitated musician rises from the piano evidently anticipating praise, you see that it was all done in
earnest.

The same thing takes place at all the concerts, with pieces
by Liszt, Wagner, Berlioz, Brahms, and (newest of all) Richard
Strauss, and the numberless other composers of the new school

15 "The quicker it goes the longer it lasts."—TR.

who unceasingly produce opera after opera, symphony after symphony, piece after piece.

The same is occurring in a domain in which it seemed hard to be unintelligible—in the sphere of novels and short stories.

Read *Là-Bas* by Huysmans, or some of Kipling's short stories, or "L'Annonciateur" by Villiers de l'Isle Adam in his *Contes Cruels,* etc., and you will find them not only "abscons" (to use a word adopted by the new writers), but absolutely unintelligible both in form and in substance. Such, again, is the work by E. Morel, "Terre Promise," now appearing in the *Revue Blanche,* and such are most of the new novels. The style is very high-flown, the feelings seem to be most elevated, but you can't make out what is happening, to whom it is happening, and where it is happening. And such is the bulk of the young art of our time.

People who grew up in the first half of this century admiring Goethe, Schiller, Musset, Hugo, Dickens, Beethoven, Chopin, Raphael, da Vinci, Michael Angelo, Delaroche, being unable to make head or tail of this new art, simply attribute its productions to tasteless insanity and wish to ignore them. But such an attitude toward this art is quite unjustifiable, because, in the first place, that art is spreading more and more and has already conquered for itself a firm position in society, similar to the one occupied by the Romanticists in the third decade of this century; and secondly and chiefly, because, if it is permissible to judge in this way of the productions of the latest form of art called by us Decadent art merely because we do not understand it, then remember there are an enormous number of people—all the laborers and many of the nonlaboring folk—who, in just the same way, do not comprehend those productions of art which we consider admirable: the verses of our favorite artists—Goethe, Schiller, and Hugo; the novels of Dickens, the music of Beethoven and Chopin, the pictures of Raphael, Michael Angelo, da Vinci, etc.

If I have a right to think that great masses of people do not understand and do not like what I consider undoubtedly good because they are not sufficiently developed, then I have no right to deny that perhaps the reason why I cannot understand and cannot like the new productions of art is merely that I am still insufficiently developed to understand them. If I have a right to say that I, and the majority of people who are in sympathy with me, do not understand the productions of the new art simply because there is nothing in it to understand and because it is bad art, then, with just the same right, the still larger majority, the whole laboring mass, who do not understand what I consider admirable art, can say that what I reckon as good art is bad art, and there is nothing in it to understand.

I once saw the injustice of such condemnation of the new art with special clearness when in my presence a certain poet who writes incomprehensible verses ridiculed incomprehensible music with gay self-assurance; and shortly afterwards, a certain musician who composes incomprehensible symphonies laughed at incomprehensible poetry with equal self-confidence. I have no right, and no authority, to condemn the new art on the ground that I (a man educated in the first half of the century) do not understand it; I can only say that it is incomprehensible to me. The only advantage the art I acknowledge has over the Decadent art lies in the fact that the art I recognize is comprehensible to a somewhat larger number of people than the present-day art.

The fact that I am accustomed to a certain exclusive art and can understand it, but am unable to understand another still more exclusive art, does not give me a right to conclude that my art is the real true art, and that the other one which I do not understand is an unreal, a bad art. I can only conclude that art, becoming ever more and more exclusive, has become more and more incomprehensible to an ever increasing number of people, and that in this its progress toward greater and greater incomprehensibility (on one level of which I am standing, with the art familiar to me), it has reached a point where it is understood by a very small number of the elect, and the number of these chosen people is ever becoming smaller and smaller.

As soon as ever the art of the upper classes separated itself from universal art, a conviction arose that art may be art and yet be incomprehensible to the masses. And as soon as this position was admitted, it had inevitably to be admitted also that art may be intelligible only to the very smallest number of the elect, and, eventually, to two, or to one, of our nearest friends, or to oneself alone, which is practically what is being said by modern artists: "I create and understand myself, and if any one does not understand me, so much the worse for him."

The assertion that art may be good art and at the same time incomprehensible to a great number of people is extremely unjust, and its consequences are ruinous to art itself; but at the same time it is so common and has so eaten into our conceptions that it is impossible sufficiently to elucidate all the absurdity of it.

Nothing is more common than to hear it said of reputed works of art that they are very good but very difficult to understand. We are quite used to such assertions, and yet to say that a work of art is good but incomprehensible to the majority of men is the same as saying of some kind of food that it is very good, but that most people can't eat it. The majority of men may not like rotten chesse or putrefying grouse—dishes esteemed by people with perverted tastes; but bread and fruit are only good when they please the majority of men. And it is the same with art. Perverted art may not please the majority of men, but good art always pleases everyone.

It is said that the very best works of art are such that they cannot be understood by the mass, but are accessible only to the elect who are prepared to understand these great works. But if the majority of men do not understand, the knowledge necessary to enable them to understand should be taught and explained to them. But it turns out that there is no such knowledge, that the works cannot be explained, and that those who say the majority do not understand good works of art still do not explain those works but only tell us that, in order to understand them, one must read, and see, and hear these same works over and over again. But this is not to explain; it is only to habituate! And people may habituate themselves to anything, even to the very worst things. As people may habituate themselves to bad food, to spirits, tobacco, and opium, just in the same way they may habituate themselves to bad art—and that is exactly what is being done.

Moreover, it cannot be said that the majority of people lack the taste to esteem the highest works of art. The majority always has understood, and still understands, what we also recognize as being the very best art: the epic of Genesis, the gospel parables, folk legends, fairy tales, and folk songs are understood by all. How can it be that the majority has suddenly lost its capacity to understand what is high in our art?

Of a speech it may be said that it is admirable, but incomprehensible to those who do not know the language in which it is delivered. A speech delivered in Chinese may be excellent and may yet remain incomprehensible to me if I do not know Chinese; but what distinguishes a work of art from all other mental activity is just the fact that its language is understood by all, and that it infects all without distinction. The tears and laughter of a Chinese infect me just as the laughter and tears of a Russian; and it is the same with painting and music and poetry when it is translated into a language I understand. The songs of a Kirghiz or of a Japanese touch me, though in a lesser degree than they touch a Kirghiz or a Japanese. I am also touched by Japanese painting, Indian architecture, and Arabian stories. If I am but little touched by a Japanese song and a Chinese novel, it is not that I do not understand these productions but that I know and am accustomed to higher works of art. It is not because their art is above me. Great works of art are only great because they are accessible and comprehensible to everyone. The story of Joseph, translated into the Chinese language, touches a Chinese. The story of Sakya Muni touches us. And there are, and must be, buildings, pictures, statues, and music of similar power. So that, if art fails to move men, it cannot be said that this is due to the spectators' or hearers' lack of understanding; but the conclusion to be drawn may and should be that such art is either bad art or is not art at all.

Art is differentiated from activity of the understanding, which demands preparation and a certain sequence of knowledge (so that one cannot learn trigonometry before knowing geometry), by the fact that it acts on people independently of their state of development and education, that the charm of a picture, sounds, or of forms, infects any man whatever his plane of development.

The business of art lies just in this—to make that understood and felt which, in the form of an argument, might be incomprehensible and inaccessible. Usually it seems to the recipient of a truly artistic impression that he knew the thing before but had been unable to express it.

And such has always been the nature of good, supreme art; the *Iliad,* the *Odyssey,* the stories of Isaac, Jacob, and Joseph, the Hebrew prophets, the psalms, the gospel parables, the story of Sakya Muni, and the hymns of the Vedas: all transmit very elevated feelings and are nevertheless quite comprehensible now to us, educated or uneducated, as they were comprehensible to the men of those times, long ago, who were even less educated than our laborers. People talk about incomprehensibility; but if art is the transmission of feelings flowing from man's religious perception, how can a feeling be incomprehensible which is founded on religion, i.e., on man's relation to God? Such art should be, and has actually always been, comprehensible to everybody because every man's relation to God is one and the same. And therefore the churches and the images in them are always comprehensible to everyone. The hindrance to understanding the best and highest feelings (as is said in the gospel) does not at all lie in deficiency of development or learning, but, on the contrary, in false development and false learning. A good and lofty work of art may be incomprehensible, but not to simple, unperverted peasant laborers (all that is highest is understood by them)—it may be, and often is, unintelligible to erudite, perverted people destitute of religion. And this continually occurs in our society in which the highest feelings are simply not understood. For instance, I know people who consider themselves most refined and who say that they do not understand the poetry of love to one's neighbor, of self-sacrifice, or of chastity.

So good, great, universal, religious art may be incomprehensible to a small circle of spoiled people but certainly not to any large number of plain men.

Art cannot be incomprehensible to the great masses only because it is very good—as artists of our day are fond of telling us. Rather we are bound to conclude that this art is unintelligible to the great masses only because it is very bad art, or even is not art at all. So that the favorite argument (naïvely accepted by the cultured crowd), that in order to feel art one has first to understand it (which really only means habituate oneself to it), is the truest indication that what we are asked to understand by such a method is either very bad, exclusive art, or is not art at all.

People say that works of art do not please the people because they are incapable of understanding them. But if the aim of works of art is to infect people with the emotion the artist has experienced, how can one talk about not understanding?

A man of the people reads a book, sees a picture, hears a play or a symphony, and is touched by no feeling. He is told that this is because he cannot understand. People promise to let a man see a certain show; he enters and sees nothing. He is told that this is because his sight is not prepared for this show. But the man well knows that he sees quite well, and if he does not see what people promised to show him, he only concludes (as is quite just) that those who undertook to show him the spectacle have not fulfilled their engagement. And it is perfectly just for a man who does feel the influence of some works of art to come to this conclusion concerning artists who do not, by their works, evoke feeling in him. To say that the reason a man is not touched by my art is because he is still too stupid, besides being very self-conceited and also rude, is to reverse the roles and for the sick to send the hale to bed.

Voltaire said that *"Tous les genres sont bons, hors le genre ennuyeux;"* [16] but with even more right one may say of art that *tous les genres sont bons, hors celui qu'on ne comprend pas,* or *qui ne produit pas son effect,*[17] for of what value is an article which fails to do that for which it was intended?

Mark this above all: if only it be admitted that art may be art and yet be unintelligible to anyone of sound mind, there is no reason why any circle of perverted people should not compose works tickling their own perverted feelings and comprehensible to no one but themselves and call it "art," as is actually being done by the so-called Decadents.

The direction art has taken may be compared to placing on a large circle other circles, smaller and smaller, until a cone is formed, the apex of which is no longer a circle at all. That is what has happened to the art of our times.

CHAPTER ELEVEN

BECOMING ever poorer and poorer in subject matter, and more and more unintelligible in form, that art of the upper classes in its latest productions has even lost all the characteristics of art, and has been replaced by imitations of art. Not only has upper-class art, in consequence of its separation from universal art, become poor in subject matter and bad in form, i.e., ever more and more unintelligible, it has in the course of time ceased even to be art at all, and has been replaced by counterfeits.

This has resulted from the following causes: Universal art arises only when someone of the people, having experienced a strong emotion, feels the necessity of transmitting it to others. The art of the rich classes, on the other hand, arises

16 [All styles are good except the boring style.]
17 [All styles are good except that which is not understood, or which fails to produce its effect.]

not from the artist's inner impulse but chiefly because people of the upper classes demand amusement and pay well for it. They demand from art the transmission of feelings that please them, and this demand artists try to meet. But it is a very difficult task; for people of the wealthy classes, spending their lives in idleness and luxury, desire to be continually diverted by art; and art, even the lowest, cannot be produced at will but has to generate spontaneously in the artist's inner self. And therefore, to satisfy the demands of people of the upper classes, artists have had to devise methods of producing imitations of art. And such methods have been devised.

These methods are those of (1) borrowing, (2) imitating, (3) striking (creating effects), and (4) interesting.

The first method consists in borrowing whole subjects, or merely separate features, from former works recognized by everyone as being poetical, and in so reshaping them with sundry additions that they should have an appearance of novelty.

Such works, evoking in people of a certain class memories of artistic feelings formerly experienced, produce an impression similar to art, and, provided only that they conform to other needful conditions, they pass for art among those who seek for pleasure from art. Subjects borrowed from previous works of art are usually called poetical subjects. Objects and people thus borrowed are called poetical objects and people. Thus, in our circle, all sorts of legends, sagas, and ancient traditions are considered poetical subjects. Among poetical people and objects we reckon maidens, warriors, shepherds, hermits, angels, devils of all sorts, moonlight, thunder, mountains, the sea, precipices, flowers, long hair, lions, lambs, doves, and nightingales. In general, all those objects are considered poetical which have been most frequently used by former artists in their productions.

Some forty years ago a stupid but highly cultured—*ayant beaucoup d'acquis*—lady (since deceased) asked me to listen to a novel written by herself. It began with a heroine who, in a poetic white dress and with poetically flowing hair, was reading poetry near some water in a poetic wood. The scene was in Russia, but suddenly from behind the bushes the hero appears, wearing a hat with a feather *à la Guillaume Tell* (the book specially mentioned this) and accompanied by two poetical white dogs. The authoress deemed all this highly poetical, and it might have passed muster if only it had not been necessary for the hero to speak. But as soon as the gentleman in the hat *à la Guillaume Tell* began to converse with the maiden in the white dress, it became obvious that the authoress had nothing to say but had merely been moved by poetic memories of other works, and imagined that by ringing the changes on those memories she could produce an artistic impression. But an artistic impression, i.e., infection, is only received when an author has, in the manner peculiar to himself, experienced the feeling which he transmits, and not when he passes on another man's feeling previously transmitted to him. Such poetry from poetry cannot infect people, it can only simulate a work of art, and even that only to people of perverted aesthetic taste. The lady in question being very stupid and devoid of talent, it was at once apparent how the case stood; but when such borrowing is resorted to by people who are erudite and talented and have cultivated the technique of their art, we get those borrowings from the Greek, the antique, the Christian or mythological world which have become so numerous, and which, particularly in our day, continue to increase and multiply, and are accepted by the public as works of art if only the borrowings are well mounted by means of the technique of the particular art to which they belong.

As a characteristic example of such counterfeits of art in the realm of poetry take Rostand's *Princess Lointaine,* in which there is not a spark of art but which seems very poetical to many people, and probably also to its author.

The second method of imparting a semblance of art is that which I have called imitating. The essence of this method consists in supplying details accompanying the thing described or depicted. In literary art this method consists in describing, in the minutest details, the external appearance, the faces, the clothes, the gestures, the tones, and the habitations of the characters represented, with all the occurrences met with in life. For instance, in novels and stories when one of the characters speaks we are told in what voice he spoke and what he was doing at the time. And the things said are not given so that they should have as much sense as possible, but as they are in life, disconnectedly and with interruptions and omissions. In dramatic art, besides such imitation of real speech, this method consists in having all the accessories and all the people just like those in real life. In painting, this method assimilates painting to photography and destroys the difference between them. And, strange to say, this method is used also in music: music tries to imitate, not only by its rhythm but by its sounds, the sounds which in real life accompany the thing it wishes to represent.

The third method is by action, often purely physical, on the outer senses. Work of this kind is said to be "striking," "effectful." In all arts these effects consist chiefly in contrasts—in bringing together the terrible and the tender, the beautiful and the hideous, the loud and the soft, darkness and light, the most ordinary and the most extraordinary. In verbal art, besides effects of contrast, there are also effects consisting in the description of things that have never before been described. These are usually pornographic details evoking sexual desire, or details of suffering and death evoking feelings of horror, as, for instance, when describing a murder to give a detailed medical account of the lacerated tissues, of the swellings, of the smell, quantity, and appearance of the blood. It is the same in painting: besides all kinds of other contrasts, one is coming into vogue which consists in giving careful finish to one object and being careless about all the rest. The chief and usual effects in painting are effects of light and the depiction of the horrible. In the drama, the most common effects besides contrasts are tempests, thunder, moonlight, scenes at sea or by the seashore, changes of costume, exposure of the female body, madness, murders, and death generally: the dying person exhibiting in detail all the phases of agony. In music the most usual effects are a *crescendo,* passing from the softest and simplest sounds to the loudest and most complex crash of the full orchestra; a repetition of the same sounds *arpeggio* in all the octaves and on various instruments; or that the harmony, tone, and rhythm be not at all those naturally flowing from the course of the musical thought, but such as strike one by their unexpectedness. Besides these, the commonest effects in music are produced in a purely physical manner by strength of sound, especially in an orchestra.

Such are some of the most usual effects in the various arts, but there yet remains one common to them all, namely, to convey by means of one art what it would be natural to convey by another: for instance, to make music describe (as is done by the program music of Wagner and his followers), or to make painting, the drama, or poetry, induce a frame of mind (as is aimed at by all the Decadent art).

The fourth method is that of interesting (that is, absorbing the mind) in connection with works of art. The interest may lie in an intricate plot—a method till quite recently much employed in English novels and French plays, but now going out of fashion and being replaced by authenticity, i.e., by detailed description of some historical period or some branch of contemporary life. For example, in a novel interestingness may consist in a description of Egyptian or Roman life, the life of miners, or that of the clerks in a large shop. The reader becomes interested and mistakes this interest for an artistic impression. The interest may also depend on the very method of expression, a kind of interest that has now come much into use. Both verse and prose, as well as pictures, plays, and music, are constructed so that they must be guessed like riddles, and this process of guessing again affords pleasure and gives a semblance of the feeling received from art.

It is very often said that a work of art is very good because it is poetic, or realistic, or striking, or interesting; whereas not only can neither the first, nor the second, nor the third, nor the fourth of these attributes supply a standard of excellence in art, but they have not even anything in common with art.

Poetic—means borrowed. All borrowing merely recalls to the reader, spectator, or listener some dim recollection of artistic impressions they have received from previous works of art and does not infect them with feeling which the artist has himself experienced. A work founded on something borrowed, like Goethe's *Faust*, for instance, may be very well executed and be full of mind and every beauty, but because it lacks the chief characteristic of a work of art—completeness, oneness, the inseparable unity of form and contents expressing the feeling the artist has experienced—it cannot produce a really artistic impression. In availing himself of this method, the artist only transmits the feeling received by him from a previous work of art; therefore every borrowing, whether it be of whole subjects, or of various scenes, situations, or descriptions, is but a reflection of art, a simulation of it, but not art itself. And therefore, to say that a certain production is good because it is poetic—i.e., resembles a work of art—is like saying of a coin that it is good because it resembles real money.

Equally little can imitation, realism, serve, as many people think, as a measure of the quality of art. Imitation cannot be such a measure; for the chief characteristic of art is the infection of others with the feelings the artist has experienced, and infection with a feeling is not only not identical with description of the accessories of what is transmitted, but is usually hindered by superfluous details. The attention of the receiver of the artistic impression is diverted by all these well-observed details, and they hinder the transmission of feeling even when it exists.

To value a work of art by the degree of its realism, by the accuracy of the details reproduced, is as strange as to judge of the nutritive quality of food by its external appearance. When we appraise a work according to its realism we only show that we are talking, not of a work of art, but of its counterfeit.

Neither does the third method of imitating art—by the use of what is striking or effectual—coincide with real art any better than the two former methods; for in effectfulness—the effects of novelty, of the unexpected, of contrasts, of the horrible—there is no transmission of feeling but only an action on the nerves. If an artist were to paint a bloody wound admirably, the sight of the wound would strike me, but it would not be art. One prolonged note on a powerful organ will produce a striking impression, will often even cause tears, but there is no music in it because no feeling is transmitted. Yet such physiological effects are constantly mistaken for art by people of our circle, and this not only in music but also in poetry, painting, and the drama. It is said that art has become refined. On the contrary, thanks to the pursuit of effectfulness, it has become very coarse. A new piece is brought out and accepted all over Europe, such, for instance, as *Hannele*,[1] in which play the author wishes to transmit to the spectators pity for a persecuted girl. To evoke this feeling in the audience by means of art, the author should either make one of the characters express this pity in such a way as to infect everyone, or he should describe the girl's feelings correctly. But he cannot, or will not, do this, and chooses another way, more complicated in stage management but easier for the author. He makes the girl die on the stage; and, still further to increase the physiological effect on the spectators, he extinguishes the lights in the theater, leaving the audience in the dark, and to the sound of dismal music he shows how the girl is pursued and beaten by her drunken father. The girl shrinks—screams—groans—and falls. Angels appear and carry her away. And the audience, experiencing some excitement while this is going on, are fully convinced that this is true aesthetic feeling. But there is nothing aesthetic in such excitement; for there is no infecting of man by man, but only a mingled feeling of pity for another, and of self-congratulation that it is not I who am suffering: it is like what we feel at the sight of an execution, or what the Romans felt in their circuses.

The substitution of effectfulness for aesthetic feeling is par-

---

1 [*Hanneles Himmelfahrt* by Gerhart Hauptmann.—Ed.]

ticularly noticeable in musical art—that art which by its
nature has an immediate physiological action on the nerves.
Instead of transmitting by means of a melody the feelings he
has experienced, a composer of the new school accumulates
and complicates sounds, and by now strengthening, now weakening them, he produces on the audience a physiological effect
of a kind that can be measured by an apparatus invented for
the purpose.[2] And the public mistakes this physiological effect
for the effect of art.

As to the fourth method—that of interesting—it also is frequently confounded with art. One often hears it said, not only
of a poem, a novel, or a picture, but even of a musical work,
that it is interesting. What does this mean? To speak of an
interesting work of art means either that we receive from a
work of art information new to us, or that the work is not
fully intelligible and that little by little, and with effort, we
arrive at its meaning and experience a certain pleasure in this
process of guessing it. In neither case has the interest anything in common with artistic impression. Art aims at infecting people with feeling experienced by the artist. But the
mental effort necessary to enable the spectator, listener, or
reader to assimilate the new information contained in the
work, or to guess the puzzles propounded, by distracting him
hinders the infection. And therefore the interestingness of a
work not only has nothing to do with its excellence as a work
of art, but rather hinders than assists artistic impression.

We may in a work of art meet with what is poetic, and
realistic, and striking, and interesting, but these things cannot replace the essential of art—feeling experienced by the
artist. Latterly, in upper-class art most of the objects given
out as being works of art are of the kind which only resemble
art and are devoid of its essential quality—feeling experienced
by the artist. And for the diversion of the rich such objects are

[2] An apparatus exists by means of which a very sensitive arrow, in
dependence on the tension of a muscle of the arm, will indicate the
physiological action of music on the nerves and muscles.

continually being produced in enormous quantities by the artisans of art.

Many conditions must be fulfilled to enable a man to produce a real work of art. It is necessary that he should stand on the level of the highest life-conception of his time, that he should experience feeling and have the desire and capacity to transmit it, and that he should, moreover, have a talent for some one of the forms of art. It is very seldom that all these conditions necessary to the production of true art are combined. But in order—aided by the customary methods of borrowing, imitating, introducing effects, and interesting—unceasingly to produce counterfeits of art which pass for art in our society and are well paid for, it is only necessary to have a talent for some branch of art; and this is very often to be met with. By talent I mean ability: in literary art, the ability to express one's thoughts and impressions easily and to notice and remember characteristic details; in the depictive arts, to distinguish and remember lines, forms, and colors; in music, to distinguish the intervals and to remember and transmit the sequence of sounds. And a man in our times, if only he possesses such a talent and selects some specialty after learning the methods of counterfeiting used in his branch of art—if he has patience and if his aesthetic feeling (which would render such productions revolting to him) be atrophied—may unceasingly till the end of his life turn out works which will pass for art in our society.

To produce such counterfeits, definite rules or recipes exist in each branch of art. So the talented man, having assimilated them, may produce such works *à froid,* cold drawn, without any feeling.

In order to write poems a man of literary talent needs only these qualifications: to acquire the knack, conformably with the requirements of rhyme and rhythm, of using instead of the one really suitable word ten others meaning approximately the same; to learn how to take any phrase which, to be clear, has but one natural order of words, and despite all possible dislocations still to retain some sense in it; and lastly, to be able, guided by the words required for the rhymes, to devise some semblance of thoughts, feelings, or descriptions to suit these words. Having acquired these qualifications, he may unceasingly produce poems—short or long, religious, amatory, or patriotic, according to the demand.

If a man of literary talent wishes to write a story or novel, he need only form his style—i.e., learn how to describe all that he sees—and accustom himself to remember or note down details. When he has accustomed himself to this, he can, according to his inclination or the demand, unceasingly produce novels or stories—historical, naturalistic, social, erotic, psychological, or even religious, for which latter kind a demand and fashion begins to show itself. He can take subjects from books or from the events of life and can copy the characters of the people in his book from his acquaintances.

And such novels and stories, if only they are decked out with well-observed and carefully noted details, preferably erotic ones, will be considered works of art even though they may not contain a spark of feeling experienced.

To produce art in dramatic form, a talented man, in addition to all that is required for novels and stories, must also learn to furnish his characters with as many smart and witty sentences as possible, must know how to utilize theatrical effects and how to entwine the action of his characters so that there should not be any long conversations but as much bustle and movement on the stage as possible. If the writer is able to do this, he may produce dramatic works one after another without stopping, selecting his subjects from the reports of the law courts, or from the latest society topic such as hypnotism, heredity, etc., or from deep antiquity, or even from the realms of fancy.

In the sphere of painting and sculpture it is still easier for the talented man to produce imitations of art. He need only learn to draw, paint, and model—especially naked bodies. Thus equipped he can continue to paint pictures or model statues, one after another, choosing subjects according to his bent—mythological, or religious, or fantastic, or symbolical; or he may depict what is written about in the papers—a coronation, a strike, the Turko-Grecian war, famine scenes; or, commonest of all, he may just copy anything he thinks beautiful —from naked women to copper basins.

For the production of musical art the talented man needs still less of what constitutes the essence of art, i.e., feeling wherewith to infect others: but on the other hand, he requires more physical, gymnastic labor than for any other art, unless it be dancing. To produce works of musical art, he must first learn to move his fingers on some instrument as rapidly as those who have reached the highest perfection; next, he must know how in former times polyphonic music was written, must study what are called counterpoint and fugue; and furthermore, he must learn orchestration, i.e., how to utilize the effects of the instruments. But once he has learned all this, the composer may unceasingly produce one work after another, whether program music, opera, or song (devising sounds more or less corresponding to the words), or chamber music, i.e., he may take another man's themes and work them up into definite forms by means of counterpoint and fugue. Or, what is commonest of all, he may compose fantastic music, i.e., he may take a conjunction of sounds which happens to come to hand and pile every sort of complication and ornamentation on to this chance combination.

Thus in all realms of art counterfeits of art are manufactured to a ready-made, pre-arranged recipe, and these counterfeits the public of our upper classes accepts for real art.

And this substitution of counterfeits for real works of art was the third and most important consequence of the separation of the art of the upper classes from universal art.

CHAPTER TWELVE

I N OUR society three conditions co-operate to cause the production of objects of counterfeit art. They are—(1) the
considerable remuneration of artists for their productions and
the professionalization of artists which this has produced, (2)
art criticism, and (3) schools of art.

While art was as yet undivided and only religious art was
valued and rewarded while indiscriminate art was left un-
rewarded, there were no counterfeits of art, or, if any existed,
being exposed to the criticism of the whole people, they
quickly disappeared. But as soon as that division occurred,
and the upper classes acclaimed every kind of art as good if
only it afforded them pleasure and began to reward such art
more highly than any other social activity, immediately a
large number of people devoted themselves to this activity
and art assumed quite a different character and became a
profession.

And as soon as this occurred, the chief and most precious
quality of art—its sincerity—was at once greatly weakened and
eventually quite destroyed.

The professional artist lives by his art and has continually
to invent subjects for his works—and does invent them. And
it is obvious how great a difference must exist between works
of art produced on the one hand by men such as the Jewish
prophets, the authors of the Psalms, Francis of Assisi, the
authors of the *Iliad* and *Odyssey,* of folk stories, legends, and
folk songs, many of whom not only received no remuneration
for their work but did not even attach their names to it; and,
on the other hand, works produced by court poets, dramatists
and musicians receiving honors and remuneration; and later
on by professional artists who lived by the trade, receiving
remuneration from newspaper editors, publishers, impresarios,
and in general from those agents who come between the
artists and the town public—the consumers of art.

Professionalism is the first condition of the diffusion of false, counterfeit art.

The second condition is the growth in recent times of artistic criticism, i.e., the valuation of art not by everybody and, above all, not by plain men, but by erudite, that is, by perverted and at the same time self-confident individuals.

A friend of mine, speaking of the relation of critics to artists, half jokingly defined it thus: "Critics are the stupid who discuss the wise." However partial, inexact, and rude this definition may be, it is yet partly true and is incomparably more just than the definition which considers critics to be men who can explain works of art.

"Critics explain!" What do they explain?

The artist, if a real artist, has by his work transmitted to others the feeling he experienced. What is there, then, to explain?

If a work be good as art, then the feeling expressed by the artist—be it moral or immoral—transmits itself to other people. If transmitted to others, then they feel it, and all interpretations are superfluous. If the work does not infect people, no explanation can make it contagious. An artist's work cannot be interpreted. Had it been possible to explain in words what he wished to convey, the artist would have expressed himself in words. He expressed it by his art only because the feeling he experienced could not be otherwise transmitted. The interpretation of works of art by words only indicates that the interpreter is himself incapable of feeling the infection of art. And this is actually the case; for, however strange it may seem to say so, critics have always been people less susceptible than other men to the contagion of art. For the most part they are able writers, educated and clever, but with their capacity of being infected by art quite perverted or atrophied. And therefore their writings have always largely contributed, and still contribute, to the perversion of the taste of that public which reads them and trusts them.

Artistic criticism did not exist—could not and cannot exist

—in societies where art is undivided, and where, consequently, it is appraised by the religious understanding of life common to the whole people. Art criticism grew, and could grow, only on the art of the upper classes who did not acknowledge the religious perception of their time.

Universal art has a definite and indubitable internal criterion—religious perception; upper-class art lacks this and therefore the appreciators of that art are obliged to cling to some external criterion. And they find it in "the judgments of the finest-nurtured," as an English aesthetician has phrased it, that is, in the authority of the people who are considered educated not only in this, but also in a tradition of such authorities. This tradition is extremely misleading, both because the opinions of "the finest-nurtured" are often mistaken, and also because judgments which were valid once cease to be so with the lapse of time. But the critics, having no basis for their judgments, never cease to repeat their traditions. The classical tragedians were once considered good, and therefore criticism considers them to be so still. Dante was esteemed a great poet, Raphael a great painter, Bach a great musician—and the critics, lacking a standard by which to separate good art from bad, not only consider these artists great but regard all their productions as admirable and worthy of imitation. Nothing has contributed, and still contributes, so much to the perversion of art as these authorities set up by criticism. A man produces a work of art, like every true artist expressing in his own peculiar manner a feeling he has experienced. Most people are infected by the artist's feeling; and his work becomes known. Then criticism, discussing the artist, says that the work is not bad, but all the same the artist is not a Dante, nor a Shakespeare, nor a Goethe, nor a Raphael, nor what Beethoven was in his last period. And the young artist sets to work to copy those who are held up for his imitation and he produces not only feeble works, but false works—counterfeits of art.

Thus, for instance, our Pushkin writes his short poems, "Eugene Onegin," "The Gipsies," and his stories—works all varying in quality, but all true art. But then, under the influence of false criticism extolling Shakespeare, he writes "Boris Godunoff," a cold, brain-spun work, and this production is lauded by the critics, set up as a model, and imitations of it appear: "Minin," by Ostrovsky and "Tsar Boris," by Alexey Tolstoy, and such imitations of imitations as crowd all literatures with insignificant productions. The chief harm done by the critics is this, that themselves lacking the capacity to be infected by art (and that is the characteristic of all critics; for did they not lack this they could not attempt the impossible —the interpretation of works of art), they pay most attention to, and eulogize, brain-spun, invented works, and set these up as models worthy of imitation. That is the reason they so confidently extol in literature the Greek tragedians, Dante, Tasso, Milton, Shakespeare, Goethe (almost all he wrote), and, among recent writers, Zola and Ibsen; in music, Beethoven's last period and Wagner. To justify their praise of these brain-spun, invented works, they devise entire theories (of which the famous theory of beauty is one); and not only dull but also talented people compose works in strict deference to these theories; and often even real artists, doing violence to their genius, submit to them.

Every false work extolled by the critics serves as a door through which the hypocrites of art at once crowd in.

It is solely due to the critics, who in our times still praise rude, savage, and, for us, often meaningless works of the ancient Greeks: Sophocles, Euripides, Aeschylus, and especially Aristophanes; or, of modern writers, Dante, Tasso, Milton, Shakespeare; in painting, all of Raphael, all of Michael Angelo, including his absurd "Last Judgment"; in music, the whole of Bach and the whole of Beethoven, including his last period—thanks only to them have the Ibsens, Maeterlincks, Verlaines, Mallarmés, Puvis de Chavannes, Klingers, Böcklins, Stucks, Schneiders, and in music the Wagners, Liszts, Berliozes, Brahmses, and Richard Strausses, etc., and all that immense mass of good-for-nothing imitators of these imitators become possible in our day.

As a good illustration of the harmful influence of criticism, take its relation to Beethoven. Among his innumerable hasty productions written to order, there are, notwithstanding their artificiality of form, works of true art. But he grows deaf, cannot hear, and begins to write invented, unfinished works which are consequently often meaningless and musically unintelligible. I know that musicians can imagine sounds vividly enough, and can almost hear what they read, but imaginary sounds can never replace real ones, and every composer must hear his production in order to perfect it. Beethoven, however, could not hear, could not perfect his work, and consequently published productions which are artistic ravings. But criticism, having once acknowledged him to be a great composer, seizes on just these abnormal works with special gusto and searches for extraordinary beauties in them. And, to justify its laudations (perverting the very meaning of musical art), it attributed to music the property of describing what it cannot describe. And imitators appear —an innumerable host of imitators of these abnormal attempts at artistic productions which Beethoven wrote when he was deaf.

Then Wagner appears, who at first in critical articles praises just Beethoven's last period and connects this music with Schopenhauer's mystical theory that music is the expression of Will—not of separate manifestations of will objectivized on various planes, but its very essence—which is in itself as absurd as this music of Beethoven. And afterward he composes music of his own on this theory, in conjunction with another still more erroneous system of the union of all the arts. After Wagner yet new imitators appear, diverging yet further from art: Brahms, Richard Strauss, and others.

Such are the results of criticism. But the third condition of the perversion of art, namely, art schools, is almost more harmful still.

As soon as art became not art for the whole people but for a rich class, it became a profession; as soon as it became a profession, methods were devised to teach it; people who chose this profession of art began to learn these methods, and thus professional schools sprang up: classes of rhetoric or literature in the public schools, academies for painting, conservatories for music, schools for dramatic art.

In these schools art is taught! But art is the transmission to others of a special feeling experienced by the artist. How can this be taught in schools?

No school can evoke feeling in a man, and still less can it teach him how to manifest it in the one particular manner natural to him alone. But the essence of art lies in these things.

The one thing these schools can teach is how to transmit feelings experienced by other artists in the way those other artists transmitted them. And this is just what the professional schools do teach; and such instruction not only does not assist the spread of true art, but, on the contrary, by diffusing counterfeits of art does more than anything else to deprive people of the capacity to understand true art.

In literary art people are taught how, without having anything they wish to say, to write a many-paged composition on a theme about which they have never thought, and, moreover, to write it so that it should resemble the work of an author admitted to be celebrated. This is taught in schools.

In painting, the chief training consists in learning to draw and paint from copies and models, the naked body chiefly (the very thing that is never seen and which a man occupied with real art hardly ever has to depict), and to draw and paint as former masters drew and painted. The composition of pictures is taught by giving out themes similar to those which have been treated by former acknowledged celebrities.

So also in dramatic schools, the pupils are taught to recite monologues just as tragedians, considered celebrated, declaimed them.

It is the same in music. The whole theory of music is nothing but a disconnected repetition of those methods which the acknowledged masters of composition made use of.

I have elsewhere quoted the profound remark of the Russian

artist Bruloff on art, but I cannot here refrain from repeating it because nothing better illustrates what can and what cannot be taught in the schools. Once when correcting a pupil's study, Bruloff just touched it in a few places and the poor dead study immediately became animated. "Why, you only touched it a *wee bit,* and it is quite another thing!" said one of the pupils. "Art begins where the *wee bit* begins," replied Bruloff, indicating by these words just what is most characteristic of art. The remark is true of all the arts, but its justice is particularly noticeable in the performance of music. That musical execution should be artistic, should be art, i.e., should infect, three chief conditions must be observed—there are many others needed for musical perfection: the transition from one sound to another must be interrupted or continuous; the sound must increase or diminish steadily; it must be blended with one and not with another sound; the sound must have this or that timbre, and much besides—but take the three chief conditions: the pitch, the time, and the strength of the sound. Musical execution is only then art, only then infects, when the sound is neither higher nor lower than it should be, that is, when exactly the infinitely small center of the required note is taken; when that note is continued exactly as long as is needed; and when the strength of the sound is neither more nor less than is required. The slightest deviation of pitch in either direction, the slightest increase or decrease in time, or the slightest strengthening or weakening of the sound beyond what is needed, destroys the perfection and, consequently, the infectiousness of the work. So the feeling of infection by the art of music, which seems so simple and so easily obtained, is a thing we receive only when the performer finds those infinitely minute degrees which are necessary to perfection in music. It is the same in all arts: a wee bit lighter, a wee bit darker, a wee bit higher, lower, to the right or the left—in painting; a wee bit weaker or stronger in intonation, or a wee bit sooner or later—in dramatic art; a wee bit omitted, over-emphasized, or exaggerated—in poetry, and there is no contagion. Infection is only obtained when an artist finds those infinitely minute degrees of which a work of art consists, and only to the extent to which he finds them. And it is quite impossible to teach people by external means to find these minute degrees; they can only be found when a man yields to his feeling. No instruction can make a dancer catch just the tact of the music, or a singer or a fiddler take exactly the infinitely minute center of his note, or a sketcher draw of all possible lines the only right one, or a poet find the only meet arrangement of the only suitable words. All this is found only by feeling. And therefore schools may teach what is necessary in order to produce something resembling art, but not art itself.

The teaching of the schools stops there where the *wee bit* begins—consequently where art begins.

Accustoming people to something resembling art disaccustoms them to the comprehension of real art. And that is how it comes about that none are more dull to art than those who have passed through the professional schools and been most successful in them. Professional schools produce an hypocrisy of art precisely akin to that hypocrisy of religion which is produced by theological colleges for training priests, pastors, and religious teachers generally. As it is impossible in a school to train a man so as to make a religious teacher of him, so it is impossible to teach a man how to become an artist.

Art schools are thus doubly destructive of art: first, in that they destroy the capacity to produce real art in those who have the misfortune to enter them and go through a seven or eight years' course; secondly, in that they generate enormous quantities of that counterfeit art which perverts the taste of the masses and overflows our world. In order that born artists may know the methods of the various arts elaborated by former artists, there should exist in all elementary schools such classes for drawing and music (singing) that, after passing through them, every talented scholar may, by using existing models accessible to all, be able to perfect himself in his art independently.

These three conditions—the professionalization of artists,

art criticism, and art schools—have had this effect: most people
in our times are quite unable to understand what art is, and
accept as art the grossest counterfeits of it.

CHAPTER THIRTEEN

To WHAT an extent people of our circle and time have lost
the capacity to receive real art and have become accustomed to accept as art things that have nothing in common
with it is best seen from the works of Richard Wagner which
have latterly come to be more and more esteemed, not only by
the Germans, but also by the French and the English, as the
very highest art, revealing new horizons to us.

The peculiarity of Wagner's music, as is known, consists in
this, that he considered that music should serve poetry, expressing all the shades of a poetical work.

The union of the drama with music, devised in the fifteenth
century in Italy for the revival of what they imagined to have
been the ancient Greek drama with music, is an artificial form
which had, and has, success only among the upper classes, and
that only when gifted composers such as Mozart, Weber,
Rossini, and others, drawing inspiration from a dramatic subject, yielded freely to the inspiration and subordinated the
text to the music, so that in their operas the important thing
to the audience was merely the music on a certain text and
not the text at all, which latter, even when it was utterly absurd, as, for instance, in the *Magic Flute,* still did not prevent
the music from producing an artistic impression.

Wagner wishes to correct the opera by letting music submit
to the demands of poetry and unite with it. But each art has
its own definite realm which is not identical with the realm of
other arts but merely comes in contact with them; and therefore, if the manifestation of, I will not say several, but even of
two arts—the dramatic and the musical—be united in one complete production, then the demands of the one art will make

it impossible to fulfil the demands of the other, as has always occurred in the ordinary operas where the dramatic art has submitted to, or rather yielded place to, the musical. Wagner wishes that musical art should submit to dramatic art and that both should appear in full strength. But this is impossible; for every work of art, if it be a true one, is an expression of intimate feelings of the artist, which are quite exceptional and not like anything else. Such is a musical production, and such is a dramatic work, if they be true art. And therefore, in order that a production in the one branch of art should coincide with a production in the other branch, it is necessary that the impossible should happen: that two works from different realms of art should be absolutely exceptional, unlike anything that existed before, and yet should coincide and be exactly alike.

And this cannot be, just as there cannot be two men, or even two leaves on a tree, exactly alike. Still less can two works from different realms of art, the musical and the literary, be absolutely alike. If they coincide, then either one is a work of art and the other a counterfeit, or both are counterfeits. Two live leaves cannot be exactly alike, but two artificial leaves may be. And so it is with works of art. They can only coincide completely when neither the one nor the other is art, but only cunningly devised semblances of it.

If poetry and music may be joined, as occurs in hymns, songs, and romances—(though even in these the music does not follow the changes of each verse of the text, as Wagner wants to, but the song and the music merely produce a coincident effect on the mind)—this occurs only because lyrical poetry and music have, to some extent, one and the same aim: to produce a mental condition and the conditions produced by lyrical poetry and by music can, more or less, coincide. But even in these conjunctions the center of gravity always lies in one of the two productions, so that it is one of them that produces the artistic impression while the other remains unregarded. And still less is it possible for such union to exist between epic or dramatic poetry and music.

Moreover, one of the chief conditions of artistic creation is the complete freedom of the artist from every kind of preconceived demand. And the necessity of adjusting his musical work to a work from another realm of art is a preconceived demand of such a kind as to destroy all possibility of creative power; and therefore works of this kind, adjusted to one another, are, and must be, as has always happened, not works of art but only imitations of art, like the music of a melodrama, signatures to pictures, illustrations, and librettos to operas.

And such are Wagner's productions. And a confirmation of this is to be seen in the fact that Wagner's new music lacks the chief characteristic of every true work of art—namely, such entirety and completeness that the smallest alteration in its form would disturb the meaning of the whole work. In a true work of art—poem, drama, picture, song, or symphony—it is impossible to extract one line, one scene, one figure, or one bar from its place and put it in another without infringing the significance of the whole work; just as it is impossible, without infringing the life of an organic being, to extract an organ from one place and insert it in another. But in the music of Wagner's last period, with the exception of certain parts of little importance which have an independent musical meaning, it is possible to make all kinds of transpositions, putting what was in front behind, and vice versa, without altering the musical sense. And the reason why these transpositions do not alter the sense of Wagner's music is because the sense lies in the words and not in the music.

The musical score of Wagner's later operas is like what the result would be should one of those versifiers—of whom there are now many, with tongues so broken that they can write verses on any theme to any rhymes in any rhythm, which sound as if they had a meaning— conceive the idea of illustrating by his verses some symphony or sonata of Beethoven, or some ballade of Chopin, in the following manner. To the first bars of one character, he writes verses corresponding in his opinion to those first bars. Next come some bars of a different character, and he also writes verses corresponding in his opinion to them but with no internal connection with the first verses, and, moreover, without rhymes and without rhythm. Such a production, without the music, would be exactly parallel in poetry to what Wagner's operas are in music, if heard without the words.

But Wagner is not only a musician, he is also a poet, or both together; and therefore, to judge of Wagner, one must know his poetry also—that same poetry which the music has to subserve. The chief poetical production of Wagner is *The Nibelungen Ring*. This work has attained such enormous importance in our time, and has such influence on all that now professes to be art, that it is necessary for every one today to have some idea of it. I have carefully read through the four booklets which contain this work, and have drawn up a brief summary of it which I give in Appendix III. I would strongly advise the reader (if he has not perused the poem itself, which would be the best thing to do) at least to read my account of it, so as to have an idea of this extraordinary work. It is a model work of counterfeit art, so gross as to be even ridiculous.

But we are told that it is impossible to judge of Wagner's works without seeing them on the stage. The second day of this drama, which, as I was told, is the best part of the whole work, was given in Moscow last winter and I went to see the performance.

When I arrived the enormous theater was already filled from top to bottom. There were grand dukes, and the flower of the aristocracy, of the merchant class, of the learned, and of the middle-class official public. Most of them held the libretto, fathoming its meaning. Musicians—some of them elderly, gray-haired men—followed the music, score in hand. Evidently the performance of this work was an event of importance.

I was rather late, but I was told that the short prelude, with which the act begins, was of little importance and that it did not matter having missed it. When I arrived, an actor sat on the stage amid decorations intended to represent a cave, before something which was meant to represent a smith's forge.

He was dressed in trico-tights and a cloak of skins, wore a wig
and an artificial beard, and with white, weak genteel hands
(his easy movements, and especially the shape of his stomach
and his lack of muscle, revealed the actor) beat an impossible
sword with an unnatural hammer in a way in which no one
ever uses a hammer; and at the same time, opening his mouth
in a strange way, he sang something incomprehensible. The
music of various instruments accompanied the strange sounds
which he emitted. From the libretto one was able to gather
that the actor had to represent a powerful dwarf who lived
in the cave and was forging a sword for Siegfried, whom he
had reared. One could tell he was a dwarf by the fact that
the actor walked all the time bending the knees of his trico-
covered legs. This dwarf, still opening his mouth in the same
strange way, long continued to sing or shout. The music
meanwhile runs over something strange, like beginnings which
are not continued and do not get finished. From the libretto
one could learn that the dwarf is telling himself about a ring
which a giant had obtained and which the dwarf wishes to
procure through Siegfried's aid, while Siegfried wants a good
sword, on the forging of which the dwarf is occupied. After
this conversation or singing to himself has gone on rather a
long time, other sounds are heard in the orchestra, also like
something beginning and not finishing, and another actor appears with a horn slung over his shoulder, accompanied by a
man running on all fours dressed up as a bear, whom he sets at
the smith-dwarf. The latter runs away without unbending
the knees of his trico-covered legs. This actor with the horn
represented the hero, Siegfried. The sounds which were
emitted in the orchestra on the entrance of this actor were intended to represent Siegfried's character, and are called Siegfried's leitmotiv. And these sounds are repeated each time
Siegfried appears. There is one fixed combination of sounds,
or leitmotiv, for each character, and this leitmotiv is repeated
every time the person whom it represents appears; and when
anyone is mentioned the motiv is heard which relates to that

person. Moreover, each article also has its own leitmotiv or chord. There is a motive of the ring, a motive of the helmet, a motive of the apple, a motive of fire, spear, sword, water, etc.; and as soon as the ring, helmet, or apple is mentioned, the motive or chord of the ring, helmet, or apple is heard. The actor with the horn opens his mouth as unnaturally as the dwarf and long continues in a chanting voice to shout some words, and in a similar chant Mime (that is the dwarf's name) answers something or other to him. The meaning of this conversation can only be discovered from the libretto; and it is that Siegfried was brought up by the dwarf, and therefore, for some reason, hates him and always wishes to kill him. The dwarf has forged a sword for Siegfried, but Siegfried is dissatisfied with it. From a ten-page conversation (by the libretto), lasting half an hour and conducted with the same strange openings of the mouth and chantings, it appears that Siegfried's mother gave birth to him in the wood, and that concerning his father all that is known is that he had a sword which was broken, the pieces of which are in Mime's possession, and that Siegfried does not know fear and wishes to go out of the wood. Mime, however, does not want to let him go. During the conversation the music never fails, at the mention of father, sword, etc., to sound the motiv of these people and things. After these conversations fresh sounds are heard— those of the god Wotan—and a wanderer appears. This wanderer is the god Wotan. Also dressed up in a wig, and also in tights, this god Wotan, standing in a stupid pose with a spear, thinks proper to recount what Mime must have known before but what it is necessary to tell the audience. He does not tell it simply, but in the form of riddles which he orders himself to guess, staking his head (one does not know why) that he will guess right. Moreover, whenever the wanderer strikes his spear on the ground, fire comes out of the ground, and in the orchestra the sounds of spear and of fire are heard. The orchestra accompanies the conversation, and the motives of the people and things spoken of are always artfully intermingled.

Besides this, the music expresses feelings in the most naïve manner: the terrible by sounds in the bass, the frivolous by rapid touches in the treble, etc.

The riddles have no meaning except to tell the audience what the nibelungs are, what the giants are, what the gods are, and what has happened before. This conversation also is chanted with strangely opened mouths and continues for eight libretto pages, correspondingly long on the stage. After this the wanderer departs and Siegfried returns and talks with Mime for thirteen pages more. There is not a single melody the whole of this time, but merely intertwinings of the leit-motivs of the people and things mentioned. The conversation tells that Mime wishes to teach Siegfried fear, and that Siegfried does not know what fear is. Having finished this conversation, Siegfried seizes one of the pieces of what is meant to represent the broken sword, saws it up, puts it on what is meant to represent the forge, melts it, and then forges it and sings "Heiho! heiho! heiho! Ho! ho! Aha! oho! aha! Heiaho! heiaho! heiaho! Ho! ho! Hahei! hoho! hahei!," and Act I finishes.

Regarding the question I had come to the theater to decide, my mind was fully made up, as surely as on the question of the merits of my lady acquaintance's novel when she read me the scene between the loose-haired maiden in the white dress and the hero with two white dogs and a hat with a feather *à la Guillaume Tell.*

From an author who could compose such spurious scenes, outraging all aesthetic feeling, as those which I had witnessed, there was nothing to be hoped; it may safely be decided that all that such an author can write will be bad because he evidently does not know what a true work of art is. I wished to leave, but the friends I was with asked me to remain, declaring that one could not form an opinion by that one act, and that the second would be better. So I stayed for the second act.

Act II, Night. Afterward, dawn. In general, the whole piece is crammed with lights, clouds, moonlight, darkness, magic fires, thunder, etc.

The scene represents a wood, and in the wood there is a

cave. At the entrance of the cave sits a third actor in tights, representing another dwarf. It dawns. Enter the god Wotan, again with a spear, and again in the guise of a wanderer. Again his sounds, together with fresh sounds of the deepest bass that can be produced. These latter indicate that the dragon is speaking. Wotan awakens the dragon. The same bass sounds are repeated, growing yet deeper and deeper. First the dragon says, "I want to sleep," but afterwards he crawls out of the cave. The dragon is represented by two men; it is dressed in a green, scaly skin, waves a tail at one end, while at the other it opens a kind of crocodile's jaw that is fastened on and from which flames appear. The dragon (who is meant to be dreadful and may appear so to five-year-old children) speaks some words in a terribly bass voice. This is all so stupid, so like what is done in a booth at a fair, that it is surprising that people over seven years of age can witness it seriously; yet thousands of quasi-cultured people sit and attentively hear and see it, and are delighted.

Siegfried, with his horn, reappears, as does Mime also. In the orchestra the sounds denoting them are emitted, and they talk about whether Siegfried does or does not know what fear is. Mime goes away, and a scene commences which is intended to be most poetical. Siegfried, in his tights, lies down in a would-be beautiful pose, and alternately keeps silent and talks to himself. He ponders, listens to the song of birds, and wishes to imitate them. For this purpose he cuts a reed with his sword and makes a pipe. The dawn grows brighter and brighter; the birds sing. Siegfried tries to imitate the birds. In the orchestra is heard the imitation of birds, alternating with sounds corresponding to the words he speaks. But Siegfried does not succeed with his pipeplaying, so he plays on his horn instead. This scene is unendurable. Of music, i.e., of art serving as a means to transmit a state of mind, experienced by the author, there is not even a suggestion. There is something that is absolutely unintelligible musically. In a musical sense a hope is continually experienced, followed by disappointment, as if a musical thought were commenced only to be broken

off. If there is something like musical beginnings, these beginnings are so short, so encumbered with complications of harmony and orchestration and with effects of contrast are so
obscure and unfinished, and what is happening on the stage
meanwhile is so abominably false, that it is difficult even to
perceive these musical snatches, let alone to be infected by
them. Above all, from the very beginning to the very end, and
in each note, the author's purpose is so audible and visible
that one sees and hears neither Siegfried nor the birds, but
only a limited, self-opinionated German, of bad taste and bad
style, who has a most false conception of poetry, and who, in
the rudest and most primitive manner, wishes to transmit to
me these false and mistaken conceptions of his.

Everyone knows the feeling of distrust and resistance which
is always evoked by an author's evident predetermination. A
narrator need only say in advance, Prepare to cry or to laugh,
and you are sure neither to cry nor to laugh. But when you
see that an author prescribes emotion at what is not touching, but only laughable or disgusting, and when you see,
moreover, that the author is fully assured that he has capti-
vated you, a painfully tormenting feeling results, similar to
what one would feel if an old, deformed woman put on a ball-
dress and smilingly coquetted before you, confident of your
approbation. This impression was strengthened by the fact
that around me I saw a crowd of three thousand people who
not only patiently witnessed all this absurd nonsense, but even
considered it their duty to be delighted with it.

I somehow managed to sit out the next scene also, in which
the monster appears to the accompaniment of his bass notes
intermingled with the motive of Siegfried; but after the fight
with the monster and all the roars, fires, and sword-wavings, I
could stand no more of it and escaped from the theater with
a feeling of repulsion which, even now, I cannot forget.

Listening to this opera, I involuntarily thought of a respected, wise, educated country laborer—one, for instance, of
those wise and truly religious men whom I know among the
peasants—and I pictured to myself the terrible perplexity such

a man would be in were he to witness what I was seeing that evening.

What would he think if he knew of all the labor spent on such a performance, and saw that audience, those great ones of the earth—old, bald-headed, gray-bearded men whom he had been accustomed to respect—sit silent and attentive, listening to and looking at all these stupidities for five hours on end? Not to speak of an adult laborer, one can hardly imagine even a child of over seven occupying himself with such a stupid, incoherent fairy tale.

And yet an enormous audience, the cream of the cultured upper classes, sits out five hours of this insane performance and goes away imagining that by paying tribute to this nonsense it has acquired a fresh right to esteem itself advanced and enlightened.

I speak of the Moscow public. But what is the Moscow public? It is but a hundredth part of that public which, while considering itself most highly enlightened, esteems it a merit to have so lost the capacity of being infected by art that not only can it witness this stupid sham without being revolted, but can even take delight in it.

In Bayreuth, where these performances were first given, people who consider themselves finely cultured assembled from the ends of the earth, spent, say, one hundred pounds each to see this performance, and for four days running they went to see and hear this nonsensical rubbish, sitting it out for six hours each day.

But why did people go, and why do they still go to these performances, and why do they admire them? The question naturally presents itself: How is the success of Wagner's works to be explained?

That success I explain to myself in this way: thanks to his exceptional position in having at his disposal the resources of a king. Wagner was able to command all the methods for counterfeiting art which have been developed by long usage, and, employing these methods with great ability, he produced a model work of counterfeit art. The reason why I have se-

lected his work for my illustration is that in no other counterfeit of art known to me are all the methods by which art is
counterfeited—namely, borrowings, imitation, effects, and interestingness—so ably and powerfully united.

From the subject, borrowed from antiquity, to the clouds
and the risings of the sun and moon, Wagner, in this work,
has made use of all that is considered poetical. We have here
the sleeping beauty, and nymphs, and subterranean fires, and
dwarfs, and battles, and swords, and love, and incest, and a
monster, and singing-birds—the whole arsenal of the poetical
is brought into action.

Moreover, everything is imitative; the decorations are imitated and the costumes are imitated. All are just as, according
to the data supplied by archaeology, they would have been in
antiquity. The very sounds are imitative; for Wagner, who
was not destitute of musical talent, invented just such sounds
as imitate the strokes of a hammer, the hissing of molten iron,
the singing of birds, etc.

Furthermore, in this work everything is in the highest degree striking in its effects and in its peculiarities: its monsters,
its magic fires, and its scenes under water; the darkness in
which the audience sits, the invisibility of the orchestra, and
the hitherto unemployed combinations of harmony.

And besides, it is all interesting. The interest lies not only
in the question who will kill whom, and who will marry
whom, and who is whose son, and what will happen next—
the interest lies also in the relation of the music to the text.
The rolling waves of the Rhine—now how is that to be expressed in music? An evil dwarf appears—how is the music to
express an evil dwarf?—and how is it to express the sensuality
of this dwarf? How will bravery, fire, or apples be expressed
in music? How are the leitmotivs of the people speaking to be
interwoven with the leitmotiv of the people and objects about
whom they speak? Besides, the music has a further interest.
It diverges from all formerly accepted laws, and most unexpected and totally new modulations crop up (as is not only

possible, but even easy in music having no inner law of its being); the dissonances are new and are allowed in a new way —and this, too, is interesting.

And it is this poeticality, imitativeness, effectfulness, and interestingness which, thanks to the peculiarities of Wagner's talent and to the advantageous position in which he was placed, are in these productions carried to the highest pitch of perfection, which act on the spectator, hypnotizing him as one would be hypnotized who should listen for several consecutive hours to the ravings of a maniac pronounced with great oratorical power.

People say, "You cannot judge without having seen Wagner performed at Bayreuth: in the dark, where the orchestra is out of sight concealed under the stage, and where the performance is brought to the highest perfection." And this just proves that we have here no question of art, but one of hypnotism. It is just what the spiritualists say. To convince you of the reality of their apparitions they usually say, "You cannot judge; you must try it, be present at several séances," i.e., come and sit silent in the dark for hours together in the same room with semi-sane people and repeat this some ten times over, and you shall see all that we see.

Yes, naturally! Only place yourself in such conditions and you may see what you will. But this can be still more quickly attained by getting drunk or smoking opium. It is the same when listening to an opera of Wagner's. Sit in the dark for four days in company with people who are not quite normal, and through the auditory nerves subject your brain to the strongest action of the sounds best adapted to excite it, and you will no doubt be reduced to an abnormal condition and be enchanted by absurdities. But to attain this end you do not even need four days; the five hours during which one "day" is enacted, as in Moscow, are quite enough. Nor are five hours needed; even one hour is enough for people who have no clear conception of what art should be, and who have come to the conclusion in advance that what they are going to see is excellent and that indifference or dissatisfaction with this work will serve as a proof of their inferiority and lack of culture.

I observed the audience present at this representation. The people who led the whole audience and gave the tone to it were those who had previously been hypnotized and who again succumbed to the hypnotic influence to which they were accustomed. These hypnotized people, being in an abnormal condition, were perfectly enraptured. Moreover, all the art critics, who lack the capacity to be infected by art and therefore always especially prize works like Wagner's opera where it is all an affair of the intellect, also, with much profundity, expressed their approval of a work affording such ample material for ratiocination. And following these two groups went that large city crowd (indifferent to art, with their capacity to be infected by it perverted and partly atrophied) headed by the princes, millionaires, and art patrons, who, like sorry harriers, keep close to those who most loudly and decidedly express their opinion.

"Oh, yes, certainly! What poetry! Marvelous! Especially the birds!" "Yes, yes! I am quite vanquished!" exclaim these people, repeating in various tones what they have just heard from men whose opinion appears to them authoritative.

If some people do feel insulted by the absurdity and spuriousness of the whole thing, they are timidly silent, as sober men are timid and silent when surrounded by tipsy ones.

And thus, thanks to the masterly skill with which it counterfeits art while having nothing in common with it, a meaningless, coarse, spurious production finds acceptance all over the world, costs millions of rubles to produce, and assists more and more to pervert the taste of people of the upper classes and their conception of what is art.

CHAPTER FOURTEEN

I KNOW that most men—not only those considered clever, but even those who are very clever and capable of understanding most difficult scientific, mathematical, or philosophic problems—can very seldom discern even the simplest and most obvious truth if it be such as to oblige them to admit the falsity of conclusions they have formed, perhaps with much difficulty —conclusions of which they are proud, which they have taught to others, and on which they have built their lives. And therefore I have little hope that what I adduce as to the perversion of art and taste in our society will be accepted or even seriously considered. Nevertheless, I must state fully the inevitable conclusion to which my investigation into the question of art has brought me. This investigation has brought me to the conviction that almost all that our society considers to be art, good art, and the whole of art, far from being real and good art, and the whole of art, is not even art at all but only a counterfeit of it. This position, I know, will seem very strange and paradoxical; but if we once acknowledge art to be a human activity by means of which some people transmit their feelings to others (and not a service of Beauty, nor a manifestation of the Idea, and so forth), we shall inevitably have to admit this further conclusion also. If it is true that art is an activity by means of which one man, having experienced a feeling, intentionally transmits it to others, then we have inevitably to admit further that of all that among us is termed the art of the upper classes—of all those novels, stories, dramas, comedies, pictures, sculptures, symphonies, operas, operettas, ballets, etc., which profess to be works of art—scarcely one in a hundred thousand proceeds from an emotion felt by its author, all the rest being but manufactured counterfeits of art in which borrowing, imitating, effects, and interestingness replace the contagion of feeling. That the proportion of real productions of art is to the counterfeits as one to some hundreds of thousands or even more may be seen by the following calculation. I have read

somewhere that the artist painters in Paris alone number
thirty thousand; there will probably be as many in England,
as many in Germany, and as many in Russia, Italy, and the
smaller states combined. So that in all there will be in Europe,
say, one hundred and twenty thousand painters; and there
are probably as many musicians and as many literary artists.
If these three hundred and sixty thousand individuals produce three works a year each (and many of them produce ten
or more), then each year yields over a million so-called works
of art. How many, then, must have been produced in the last
ten years, and how many in the whole time since upper-class
art broke off from the art of the whole people? Evidently millions. Yet who of all the connoisseurs of art has received impressions from all these pseudo works of art? Not to mention
all the laboring classes who have no conception of these productions, even people of the upper classes cannot know one in
a thousand of them all, and cannot remember those they have
known. These works all appear under the guise of art, produce no impression on anyone (except when they serve as
pastimes for the idle crowd of rich people), and vanish utterly.

In reply to this it is usually said that without this enormous
number of unsuccessful attempts we should not have the real
works of art. But such reasoning is as though a baker, in reply
to a reproach that his bread was bad, were to say that if it
were not for the hundreds of spoiled loaves there would not
be any well-baked ones. It is true that where there is gold
there is also much sand; but that cannot serve as a reason for
talking a lot of nonsense in order to say something wise.

We are surrounded by productions considered artistic.
Thousands of verses, thousands of poems, thousands of novels,
thousands of dramas, thousands of pictures, thousands of
musical pieces follow one after another. All the verses describe
love, or nature, or the author's state of mind, and in all of
them rhyme and rhythm are observed. All the dramas and
comedies are splendidly mounted and are performed by admirably trained actors. All the novels are divided into chapters; all of them describe love, contain effective situations, and

correctly describe the details of life. All the symphonies contain *allegro, andante, scherzo,* and *finale;* all consist of modulations and chords and are played by highly trained musicians. All the pictures, in gold frames, saliently depict faces and sundry accessories. But among these productions in the various branches of art there is in each branch one among hundreds of thousands, not only somewhat better than the rest, but differing from them as a diamond differs from paste. The one is priceless, the others not only have no value but are worse than valueless, for they deceive and pervert taste. And yet, externally, they are to a man of perverted or atrophied artistic perception precisely alike.

In our society the difficulty of recognizing real works of art is further increased by the fact that the external quality of the work in false productions is not only no worse, but often better, than in real ones; the counterfeit is often more effective than the real, and its subject more interesting. How is one to discriminate? How is one to find a production in no way distinguished in externals from hundreds of thousands of others intentionally made to imitate it precisely?

For a country peasant of unperverted taste this is as easy as it is for an animal of unspoiled scent to follow the trace he needs among a thousand others in wood or forest. The animal unerringly finds what it needs. So also the man, if only his natural qualities have not been perverted, will without fail select from among thousands of objects the real work of art he requires—that which infects him with the feeling experienced by the artist. But it is not so with those whose taste has been perverted by their education and life. The receptive feeling for art of these people is atrophied, and in valuing artistic productions they must be guided by discussion and study, which discussion and study completely confuse them. So that most people in our society are quite unable to distinguish a work of art from the grossest counterfeit. People sit for whole hours in concert rooms and theaters listening to the new composers, consider it a duty to read the novels of the famous modern novelists and to look at pictures representing either something incomprehensible or just the very thing they see much better in real life; and, above all, they consider it incombent on them to be enraptured by all this, imagining it all to be art, while at the same time they will pass real works of art by, not only without attention, but even with contempt, merely because in their circle these works are not included in the list of works of art.

A few days ago I was returning home from a walk feeling depressed, as occurs sometimes. On nearing the house I heard the loud singing of a large choir of peasant women. They were welcoming my daughter, celebrating her return home after her marriage. In this singing, with its cries and clanging of scythes, such a definite feeling of joy, cheerfulness, and energy was expressed that, without noticing how it infected me, I continued my way toward the house in a better mood and reached home smiling and quite in good spirits. That same evening a visitor, an admirable musician famed for his execution of classical music, and particularly of Beethoven, played us Beethoven's sonata, Opus 101. For the benefit of those who might otherwise attribute my judgment of that sonata of Beethoven to non-comprehension of it, I should mention that, whatever other people understand of that sonata and of other productions of Beethoven's later period, I, being very susceptible to music, equally understood. For a long time I used to attune myself so as to delight in those shapeless improvisations which form the subject matter of the works of Beethoven's later period, but I had only to consider the question of art seriously, and to compare the impression I received from Beethoven's later works with those pleasant, clear, and strong musical impressions which are transmitted, for instance, by the melodies of Bach (his arias), Haydn, Mozart, Chopin (when his melodies are not overloaded with complications and ornamentation), and of Beethoven himself in his earlier period, and, above all, with the impressions produced by folk songs—Italian, Norwegian, or Russian—by the Hungarian czardas and other such simple, clear, and powerful music, and the obscure, almost unhealthy excitement from

Beethoven's later pieces that I had artificially evoked in myself was immediately destroyed.

On the completion of the performance (though it was noticeable that everyone had become dull) those present, in the accepted manner, warmly praised Beethoven's profound production and did not forget to add that formerly they had not been able to understand that last period of his, but that they now saw that he was really then at his very best. And when I ventured to compare the impression made on me by the singing of the peasant women—an impression which had been shared by all who heard it—with the effect of this sonata, the admirers of Beethoven only smiled contemptuously, not considering it necessary to reply to such strange remarks.

But, for all that, the song of the peasant women was real art, transmitting a definite and strong feeling, while the 101st sonata of Beethoven was only an unsuccessful attempt at art, containing no definite feeling and therefore not infectious.

For my work on art I have this winter read diligently, though with great effort, the celebrated novels and stories, praised by all Europe, written by Zola, Bourget, Huysmans, and Kipling. At the same time I chanced on a story in a child's magazine, and by a quite unknown writer, which told of the Easter preparations in a poor widow's family. The story tells how the mother managed with difficulty to obtain some wheat flour, which she poured on the table ready to knead. She then went out to procure some yeast, telling the children not to leave the hut and to take care of the flour. When the mother had gone, some other children ran shouting near the window, calling those in the hut to come to play. The children forgot their mother's warning, ran into the street, and were soon engrossed in the game. The mother, on her return with the yeast, finds a hen on the table throwing the last of the flour to her chickens, who were busily picking it out of the dust of the earthen floor. The mother, in despair, scolds the children, who cry bitterly. And the mother begins to feel pity for them—but the white flour has all gone. So to mend matters she decides to make the Easter cake with sifted rye flour, brushing it over with white of egg, and surrounding it with eggs. "Ryebread which we bake is akin to any cake," says the mother, using a rhyming proverb to console the children for not having an Easter cake made with white flour. And the children, quickly passing from despair to rapture, repeat the proverb and await the Easter cake more merrily even than before.

Well! the reading of the novels and stories by Zola, Bourget, Huysmans, Kipling, and others, handling the most harrowing subjects, did not touch me for one moment, and I was provoked with the authors all the while, as one is provoked with a man who considers you so naïve that he does not even conceal the trick by which he intends to take you in. From the first lines you see the intention with which the book is written, and the details all become superfluous and one feels dull. Above all, one knows that the author had no other feeling all the time than a desire to write a story or a novel, and so one receives no artistic impression. On the other hand, I could not tear myself away from the unknown author's tale of the children and the chickens, because I was at once infected by the feeling which the author had evidently experienced, re-evoked in himself, and transmitted.

Vasnetsov is one of our Russian painters. He has painted ecclesiastical pictures in Kiev Cathedral, and everyone praises him as the founder of some new, elevated kind of Christian art. He worked at those pictures for ten years, was paid tens of thousands of rubles for them, and they are all simply bad imitations of imitations of imitations, destitute of any spark of feeling. And this same Vasnetsov drew a picture for Turgenev's story, "The Quail" (in which it is told how, in his son's presence, a father killed a quail and felt pity for it), showing the boy asleep with pouting upper lip, and above him, as a dream, the quail. And this picture is a true work of art.

In the English Academy of 1897 two pictures were exhibited together, one of which, by J. C. Dolman, was the temptation of St. Anthony. The saint is on his knees praying. Behind him stands a naked woman and animals of some kind. It is apparent that the naked woman pleased the artist very much, but that Anthony did not concern him at all; and that, so far from the temptation being terrible to him (the artist), it is highly agreeable. And therefore if there be any art in this picture, it is very nasty and false. Next in the same book of academy pictures comes a picture by Langley, showing a stray beggarboy who has evidently been called in by a woman who has taken pity on him. The boy, pitifully drawing his bare feet under the bench, is eating; the woman is looking on, probably considering whether he will not want some more; and a girl of about seven, leaning on her arm, is carefully and seriously looking on, not taking her eyes from the hungry boy, and evidently understanding for the first time what poverty is, and what inequality among people is, and asking herself why she has everything provided for her while this boy goes barefoot and hungry. She feels sorry, and yet pleased. And she loves both the boy and goodness. . . . And one feels that the artist loved this girl, and that she too loves. And this picture by an artist who, I think, is not very widely known is an admirable and true work of art.

I remember seeing a performance of *Hamlet* by Rossi. Both the tragedy itself and the performer who took the chief part are considered by our critics to represent the climax of supreme dramatic art. And yet, both from the subject matter of the drama and from the performance, I experienced all the time that peculiar suffering which is caused by false imitations of works of art. And I lately read of a theatrical performance among the savage tribe, the Voguls. A spectator describes the play. A big Vogul and a little one, both dressed in reindeer skins, represent a reindeer-doe and its young. A third Vogul, with a bow, represents a huntsman on snowshoes, and a fourth imitates with his voice a bird that warns the reindeer of their danger. The play is that the huntsman follows the track that the doe with its young one has traveled. The deer run off the scene, and again reappear. (Such performances take place in a small tent-house.) The huntsman gains more and more on the pursued. The little deer is tired, and presses against its mother. The doe stops to draw breath. The hunter comes up with them and draws his bow. But just then the bird sounds its note, warning the deer of their danger. They escape. Again there is a chase, and again the hunter gains on them, catches them, and lets fly his arrow. The arrow strikes the young deer. Unable to run, the little one presses against its mother. The mother licks its wound. The hunter draws another arrow. The audience, as the eyewitness describes them, are paralyzed with suspense; deep groans and even weeping is heard among them. And, from the mere description, I felt that this was a true work of art.

What I am saying will be considered irrational paradox, at which one can only be amazed; but for all that I must say what I think; namely, that people of our circle, of whom some compose verses, stories, novels, operas, symphonies, and sonatas, paint all kinds of pictures and make statues, while others hear and look at these things, and again others appraise and criticize it all, discuss, condemn, triumph, and raise monuments to one another, generation after generation—that all these people, with very few exceptions artists, and public, and critics, have never (except in childhood and earliest youth before hearing any discussions on art) experienced that simple feeling familiar to the plainest man and even to a child, that sense of infection with another's feeling, compelling us to joy in another's gladness, to sorrow at another's grief, and to mingle souls with another—which is the very essence of art. And therefore these people not only cannot distinguish true works of art from counterfeits, but continually mistake for real art the worst and most artificial, while they do not even perceive works of real art because the counterfeits are always more ornate, while true art is modest.

CHAPTER FIFTEEN

A RT, in our society, has been so perverted that not only has bad art come to be considered good, but even the very perception of what art really is has been lost. In order to be able to speak about the art of our society, it is, therefore, first of all necessary to distinguish art from counterfeit art.

There is one indubitable indication distinguishing real art from its counterfeit, namely, the infectiousness of art. If a man, without exercising effort and without altering his standpoint on reading, hearing, or seeing another man's work, experiences a mental condition which unites him with that man and with other people who also partake of that work of art, then the object evoking that condition is a work of art. And however poetical, realistic, effectful, or interesting a work may be, it is not a work of art if it does not evoke that feeling (quite distinct from all other feelings) of joy and of spiritual union with another (the author) and with others (those who are also infected by it).

It is true that this indication is an *internal* one, and that there are people who have forgotten what the action of real art is, who expect something else from art (in our society the great majority are in this state), and that therefore such people may mistake for this aesthetic feeling the feeling of diversion and a certain excitement which they receive from counterfeits of art. But though it is impossible to undeceive these people, just as it is impossible to convince a man suffering from "Daltonism" [1] that green is not red, yet, for all that, this indication remains perfectly definite to those whose feeling for art is neither perverted nor atrophied, and it clearly distinguishes the feeling produced by art from all other feelings.

The chief peculiarity of this feeling is that the receiver of a true artistic impression is so united to the artist that he feels

[1] [A kind of color blindness discovered by John Dalton.—Ed.]

as if the work were his own and not someone else's—as if what it expresses were just what he had long been wishing to express. A real work of art destroys, in the consciousness of the receiver, the separation between himself and the artist—not that alone, but also between himself and all whose minds receive this work of art. In this freeing of our personality from its separation and isolation, in this uniting of it with others, lies the chief characteristic and the great attractive force of art.

If a man is infected by the author's condition of soul, if he feels this emotion and this union with others, then the object which has effected this is art; but if there be no such infection, if there be not this union with the author and with others who are moved by the same work—then it is not art. And not only is infection a sure sign of art, but the degree of infectiousness is also the sole measure of excellence in art.

The stronger the infection, the better is the art as art, speaking now apart from its subject matter, i.e., not considering the quality of the feelings it transmits.

And the degree of the infectiousness of art depends on three conditions:

(1) On the greater or lesser individuality of the feeling transmitted;
(2) on the greater or lesser clearness with which the feeling is transmitted;
(3) on the sincerity of the artist, i.e., on the greater or lesser force with which the artist himself feels the emotion he transmits.

The more individual the feeling transmitted the more strongly does it act on the receiver; the more individual the state of soul into which he is transferred, the more pleasure does the receiver obtain, and therefore the more readily and strongly does he join in it.

The clearness of expression assists infection because the receiver, who mingles in consciousness with the author, is the better satisfied the more clearly the feeling is transmitted, which, as it seems to him, he has long known and felt, and for which he has only now found expression.

But most of all is the degree of infectiousness of art increased by the degree of sincerity in the artist. As soon as the spectator, hearer, or reader feels that the artist is infected by his own production, and writes, sings, or plays for himself, and not merely to act on others, this mental condition of the artist infects the receiver; and contrariwise, as soon as the spectator, reader, or hearer feels that the author is not writing, singing, or playing for his own satisfaction—does not himself feel what he wishes to express—but is doing it for him, the receiver, a resistance immediately springs up, and the most individual and the newest feelings and the cleverest technique not only fail to produce any infection but actually repel.

I have mentioned three conditions of contagiousness in art, but they may be all summed up into one, the last, sincerity, i.e., that the artist should be impelled by an inner need to express his feeling. That condition includes the first; for if the artist is sincere he will express the feeling as he experienced it. And as each man is different from everyone else, his feeling will be individual for everyone else; and the more individual it is—the more the artist has drawn it from the depths of his nature—the more sympathetic and sincere will it be. And this same sincerity will impel the artist to find a clear expression of the feeling which he wishes to transmit.

Therefore this third condition—sincerity—is the most important of the three. It is always complied with in peasant art, and this explains why such art always acts so powerfully; but it is a condition almost entirely absent from our upper-class art, which is continually produced by artists actuated by personal aims of covetousness or vanity.

Such are the three conditions which divide art from its counterfeits, and which also decide the quality of every work of art apart from its subject matter.

The absence of any one of these conditions excludes a work from the category of art and relegates it to that of art's counterfeits. If the work does not transmit the artist's peculiarity of feeling and is therefore not individual, if it is unintelligibly expressed, or if it has not proceeded from the author's inner need for expression—it is not a work of art. If all these conditions are present, even in the smallest degree, then the work, even if a weak one, is yet a work of art.

The presence in various degrees of these three conditions—individuality, clearness, and sincerity—decides the merit of a work of art as art, apart from subject matter. All works of art take rank of merit according to the degree in which they fulfil the first, the second, and the third of these conditions. In one the individuality of the feeling transmitted may predominate; in another, clearness of expression; in a third, sincerity; while a fourth may have sincerity and individuality but be deficient in clearness; a fifth, individuality and clearness but less sincerity; and so forth, in all possible degrees and combinations.

Thus is art divided from that which is not art, and thus is the quality of art as art decided, independently of its subject matter, i.e., apart from whether the feelings it transmits are good or bad.

But how are we to define good and bad art with reference to its subject matter?

CHAPTER SIXTEEN

How are we to decide what is good or bad in the subject matter of art?

Art, like speech, is a means of communication, and therefore of progress, i.e., of the movement of humanity forward toward perfection. Speech renders accessible to men of the latest generations all the knowledge discovered by the experience and reflection, both of preceding generations and of the best and foremost men of their own times; art renders accessible to men of the latest generations all the feelings experienced by their predecessors, and those also which are being felt by their best and foremost contemporaries. And as the evolution of knowledge proceeds by truer and more necessary knowledge, dislodging and replacing what is mistaken and unnecessary, so the evolution of feeling proceeds through art—feelings less kind and less needful for the well-being of mankind are replaced by others kinder and more needful for that end. That is the purpose of art. And, speaking now of its subject matter, the more art fulfills that purpose the better the art, and the less it fulfils it, the worse the art.

And the appraisement of feelings (i.e., the acknowledgment of these or those feelings as being more or less good, more or less necessary for the well-being of mankind) is made by the religious perception of the age.

In every period of history, and in every human society, there exists an understanding of the meaning of life which represents the highest level to which men of that society have attained, an understanding defining the highest good at which that society aims. And this understanding is the religious perception of the given time and society. And this religious perception is always clearly expressed by some advanced men, and more or less vividly perceived by all the members of the society. Such a religious perception and its corresponding expression exists always in every society. If it appears to us that in our society there is no religious perception, this is not because there really is none, but only because we do not want to see it. And we often wish not to see it because it exposes the fact that our life is inconsistent with that religious perception.

Religious perception in a society is like the direction of a flowing river. If the river flows at all, it must have a direction. If a society lives, there must be a religious perception indicating the direction in which, more or less consciously, all its members tend.

And so there always has been, and there is, a religious perception in every society. And it is by the standard of this religious perception that the feelings transmitted by art have always been estimated. Only on the basis of this religious perception of their age have men always chosen from the end-

lessly varied spheres of art that art which transmitted feelings
making religious perception operative in actual life. And such
art has always been highly valued and encouraged, while art
transmitting feelings already outlived, flowing from the antiquated religious perceptions of a former age, has always been
condemned and despised. All the rest of art, transmitting
those most diverse feelings by means of which people commune together, was not condemned, and was tolerated, if only
it did not transmit feelings contrary to religious perception.
Thus, for instance, among the Greeks art transmitting the
feeling of beauty, strength, and courage (Hesiod, Homer,
Phidias) was chosen, approved, and encouraged, while art
transmitting feelings of rude sensuality, despondency, and effeminacy was condemned and despised. Among the Jews, art
transmitting feelings of devotion and submission to the God
of the Hebrews and to His will (the epic of Genesis, the
prophets, the Psalms) was chosen and encouraged, while art
transmitting feelings of idolatry (the golden calf) was condemned and despised. All the rest of art—stories, songs, dances,
ornamentation of houses, of utensils, and of clothes—which
was not contrary to religious perception was neither distinguished nor discussed. Thus, in regard to its subject matter,
has art been appraised always and everywhere, and thus it
should be appraised; for this attitude toward art proceeds
from the fundamental characteristics of human nature, and
those characteristics do not change.

I know that according to an opinion current in our times
religion is a superstition which humanity has outgrown, and
that it is therefore assumed that no such thing exists as a religious perception, common to us all, by which art, in our
time, can be evaluated. I know that this is the opinion current
in the pseudo-cultured circles of today. People who do not
acknowledge Christianity in its true meaning because it un-
dermines all their social privileges, and who, therefore, invent
all kinds of philosophic and aesthetic theories to hide from
themselves the meaninglessness and wrongness of their lives,
cannot think otherwise. These people intentionally, or some-

times unintentionally, confusing the conception of a religious cult with the conception of religious perception think that by denying the cult they get rid of religious perception. But even the very attacks on religion and the attempts to establish a life-conception contrary to the religious perception of our times most clearly demonstrate the existence of a religious perception condemning the lives that are not in harmony with it.

If humanity progresses, i.e., moves forward, there must inevitably be a guide to the direction of that movement. And religions have always furnished that guide. All history shows that the progress of humanity is accomplished not otherwise than under the guidance of religion. But if the race cannot progress without the guidance of religion—and progress is always going on, and consequently also in our own times—then there must be a religion of our times. So that, whether it pleases or displeases the so-called cultured people of today, they must admit the existence of religion—not of a religious cult, Catholic, Protestant, or another, but of religious perception—which, even in our times, is the guide always present where there is any progress. And if a religious perception exists among us, then our art should be appraised on the basis of that religious perception; and, as has always and everywhere been the case, art transmitting feelings flowing from the religious perception of our time should be chosen from all the indifferent art, should be acknowledged, highly esteemed, and encouraged, while art running counter to that perception should be condemned and despised, and all the remaining indifferent art should neither be distinguished nor encouraged.

The religious perception of our time, in its widest and most practical application, is the consciousness that our well-being, both material and spiritual, individual and collective, temporal and eternal, lies in the growth of brotherhood among all men—in their loving harmony with one another. This perception is not only expressed by Christ and all the best men of past ages, it is not only repeated in the most varied forms and from most diverse sides by the best men of our own times, but it already serves as a clue to all the complex labor of humanity, consisting as this labor does, on the one hand, in the destruction of physical and moral obstacles to the union of men, and, on the other hand, in establishing the principles common to all men which can and should unite them into one universal brotherhood. And it is on the basis of this perception that we should appraise all the phenomena of our life, and, among the rest, our art also; choosing from all its realms whatever transmits feelings flowing from this religious perception, highly prizing and encouraging such art, rejecting whatever is contrary to this perception, and not attributing to the rest of art an importance not properly pertaining to it.

The chief mistake made by people of the upper classes of the time of the so-called Renaissance—a mistake which we still perpetuate—was not that they ceased to value and to attach importance to religious art (people of that period could not attach importance to it, because, like our own upper classes, they could not believe in what the majority considered to be religion), but their mistake was that they set up in place of religious art, which was lacking, an insignificant art which aimed only at giving pleasure, i.e., they began to choose, to value, and to encourage in place of religious art something which in any case did not deserve such esteem and encouragement.

One of the Fathers of the Church said that the great evil is not that men do not know God, but that they have set up, instead of God, that which is not God. So also with art. The great misfortune of the people of the upper classes of our time is not so much that they are without a religious art as such; instead of a supreme religious art, chosen from all the rest as being specially important and valuable, they have chosen a most insignificant and, usually, harmful art which aims at pleasing certain people and which, therefore, if only by its exclusive nature, stands in contradiction to that Christian priciple of universal union which forms the religious perception of our time. Instead of religious art, an empty and often vicious art is set up, and this hides from men's notice the need of that true religious art which should be present in order to improve life.

It is true that art which satisfies the demands of the religious perception of our time is quite unlike former art, but, notwithstanding this dissimilarity, to a man who does not intentionally hide the truth from himself, it is very clear and definite what does form the religious art of our age. In former times, when the highest religious perception united only some people (who, even if they formed a large society, were yet but one society surrounded by others—Jews, or Athenian, or Roman citizens), the feelings transmitted by the art of that time flowed from a desire for the might, greatness, glory, and prosperity of that society, and the heroes of art might be people who contributed to that prosperity by strength, by craft, by fraud, or by cruelty (Ulysses, Jacob, David, Samson, Hercules, and all the heroes). But the religious perception of our times does not select any one society of men; on the contrary, it demands the union of all—absolutely of all people without exception—and above every other virtue it sets brotherly love to all men. And therefore, the feelings transmitted by the art of our time not only cannot coincide with the feelings transmitted by former art, but must run counter to them.

Christian, truly Christian, art has been so long in establishing itself, and has not yet established itself, just because the Christian religious perception was not one of those small steps by which humanity advances regularly, but was an enormous revolution, which, if it has not already altered, must inevitably alter the entire life-conception of mankind, and, consequently, the whole internal organization of their life. It is true that the life of humanity, like that of an individual, moves regularly; but in that regular movement come, as it were, turning points which sharply divide the preceding from the subsequent life. Christianity was such a turning point; such, at least, it must appear to us who live by the Christian perception of life. Christian perception gave another, a new, direction to all human feelings, and therefore completely altered both the contents and the significance of art. The Greeks could make use of Persian art and the Romans could use Greek art, or, similarly, the Jews could use Egyptian art—the fundamental ideals were one and the same. Now the ideal was the greatness and prosperity of the Persians, now the greatness and prosperity of the Greeks, now that of the Romans. The same art was transferred into other conditions and served new nations. But the Christian ideal changed and reversed everything, so that, as the gospel puts it, "That which was exalted among men has become an abomination in the sight of God." The ideal is no longer the greatness of Pharaoh or of a Roman emperor, not the beauty of a Greek nor the wealth of Phoenicia, but humility, purity, compassion, love. The hero is no longer Dives,[1] but Lazarus the beggar; not Mary Magdalene in the day of her beauty, but in the day of her repentance; not those who acquire wealth, but those who have abandoned it; not those who dwell in palaces, but those who dwell in catacombs and huts; not those who rule over others, but those who acknowledge no authority but God's. And the greatest work of art is no longer a cathedral of victory [2] with statues of conquerors, but the representation of a human soul so transformed by love that a man who is tormented and murdered yet pities and loves his persecutors.

And the change is so great that men of the Christian world find it difficult to resist the inertia of the heathen art to which they have been accustomed all their lives. The subject matter of Christian religious art is so new to them, so unlike the subject matter of former art, that it seems to them as though Christian art were a denial of art, and they cling desperately to the old art. But this old art, having no longer in our day

---

[1] [Reference is apparently to Publius Linius Crassus, a contemporary of Julius Caesar who was called "Dives." But there is a play with words. It also means "rich," sumptuous, or striving for material goods as the major goal of life.—ED.]

[2] There is in Moscow a magnificent "Cathedral of our Saviour," erected to commemorate the defeat of the French in the war of 1812.—TR.

any source in religious perception, has lost its meaning and we shall have to abandon it whether we wish to or not.

The essence of the Christian perception consists in the recognition by every man of his sonship to God and of the consequent union of men with God and with one another, as is said in the gospel (John xvii. 21 [3]). Therefore the subject matter of Christian art is such feeling as can unite men with God and with one another.

The expression *unite men with God and with one another* may seem obscure to people accustomed to the misuse of these words which is so customary, but the words have a perfectly clear meaning, nevertheless. They indicate that the Christian union of man (in contradiction to the partial, exclusive union of only some men) is that which unites all without exception.

Art, all art, has this characteristic, that it unites people. Every art causes those to whom the artist's feeling is transmitted to unite in soul with the artist, and also with all who receive the same impression. But non-Christian art, while uniting some people together, makes that very union a cause of separation between these united people and others; so that union of this kind is often a source, not only of division, but even of enmity toward others. Such is all patriotic art, with its anthems, poems, and monuments; such is all Church art, i.e., the art of certain cults, with their images, statues, processions, and other local ceremonies. Such art is belated and non-Christian art, uniting the people of one cult only to separate them yet more sharply from the members of other cults, and even to place them in relations of hostility to each other. Christian art is only such as tends to unite all without exception, either by evoking in them the perception that each man and all men stand in like relation toward God and toward their neighbor, or by evoking in them identical feelings which may even be the very simplest, provided only that they are not repugnant to Christianity and are natural to everyone without exception.

[3] "That they all may be one; as thou, Father, art in me, and I in thee, that they also may be one in us."

Good Christian art of our time may be unintelligible to people because of imperfections in its form or because men are inattentive to it, but it must be such that all men can experience the feelings it transmits. It must be the art, not of some one group of people, nor of one class, nor of one nationality, nor of one religious cult; that is, it must not transmit feelings which are accessible only to a man educated in a certain way, or only to an aristocrat, or a merchant, or only to a Russian, or a native of Japan, or a Roman Catholic, or a Buddhist, etc., but it must transmit feelings accessible to everyone. Only art of this kind can be acknowledged in our time to be good art, worthy of being chosen out from all the rest of art and encouraged.

Christian art, i.e., the art of our time, should be catholic in the original meaning of the word, i.e., universal, and therefore it should unite all men. And only two kinds of feeling do unite all men: first, feelings flowing from the perception of our sonship to God and of the brotherhood of man; and next, the simple feelings of common life, accessible to every one without exception—such as the feeling of merriment, of pity, of cheerfulness, of tranquillity, etc. Only these two kinds of feelings can now supply material for art good in its subject matter.

And the action of these two kinds of art, apparently so dissimilar, is one and the same. The feelings flowing from perception of our sonship to God and of the brotherhood of man —such as a feeling of sureness in truth, devotion to the will of God, self-sacrifice, respect for and love of man—evoked by Christian religious perception; and the simplest feelings—such as a softened or a merry mood caused by a song or an amusing jest intelligible to everyone, or by a touching story, or a drawing, or a little doll: both alike produce one and the same effect, the loving union of man with man. Sometimes people who are together are, if not hostile to one another, at least estranged in mood and feeling till perchance a story, a performance, a picture, or even a building, but most often of all music, unites them all as by an electric flash, and in place of their former isolation or even enmity they are all conscious of union and mutual love. Each is glad that another feels what he feels; glad of the communion established, not only between him and all present, but also with all now living who will yet share the same impression; and more than that, he feels the mysterious gladness of a communion which, reaching beyond the grave, unites us with all men of the past who have been moved by the same feelings, and with all men of the future who will yet be touched by them. And this effect is produced both by the religious art which transmits feelings of love to God and one's neighbor and by universal art transmitting the very simplest feelings common to all men.

The art of our time should be appraised differently from former art chiefly in this, that the art of our time, i.e., Christian art (basing itself on a religious perception which demands the union of man), excludes from the domain of art good in subject matter everything transmitting exclusive feelings which do not unite, but divide, men. It relegates such work to the category of art bad in its subject matter, while, on the other hand, it includes in the category of art good in subject matter a section not formerly admitted to deserve to be chosen out and respected, namely, universal art, transmitting even the most trifling and simple feelings if only they are accessible to all men without exception and therefore unite them. Such art cannot in our time but be esteemed good, for it attains the end which the religious perception of our time, i.e., Christianity, sets before humanity.

Christian art either evokes in men those feelings which, through love of God and of one's neighbor, draw them to greater and ever greater union and make them ready for and capable of such union, or evokes in them those feelings which show them that they are already united in the joys and sorrows of life. And therefore the Christian art of our time can be and is of two kinds: (1) art transmitting feelings flowing from a religious perception of man's position in the world in relation to God and to his neighbor—religious art in the limited meaning of the term; and (2) art transmitting the simplest feelings of common life, but such, always, as are accessible to all men in the whole world: the art of common life —the art of a people—universal art. Only these two kinds of art can be considered good art in our time.

The first, religious art—transmitting both positive feelings of love of God and one's neighbor, and negative feelings of indignation and horror at the violation of love—manifests itself chiefly in the form of words and to some extent also in painting and sculpture; the second kind (universal art), transmitting feelings accessible to all, manifests itself in words, in painting, in sculpture, in dances, in architecture, and, most of all, in music.

If I were asked to give modern examples of each of these kinds of art, then, as examples of the highest art flowing from love of God and man (both of the higher, positive, and of the lower, negative kind), in literature I should name *The Robbers* by Schiller; Victor Hugo's *Les Pauvres Gens* and *Les Misérables*; the novels and stories of Dickens, *The Tale of Two Cities, The Christmas Carol, The Chimes,* and others; *Uncle Tom's Cabin;* Dostoevsky's works, especially his *Memoirs from the House of Death;* and *Adam Bede* by George Eliot.

In modern painting, strange to say, works of this kind directly transmitting the Christian feeling of love of God and of one's neighbor are hardly to be found, especially among the works of the celebrated painters. There are plenty of pictures treating of the gospel stories; they, however, depict historical events with great wealth of detail, but do not, and cannot, transmit religious feeling not possessed by their painters. There are many pictures treating of the personal feelings of various people, but of pictures representing great deeds of self-sacrifice and of Christian love there are very few, and what there are, are principally by artists who are not celebrated and are for the most part not pictures, but merely sketches. Such, for instance, is the drawing by Kramskoy (worth many of his finished pictures), showing a drawing room with a balcony, past which troops are marching in triumph on their return from the war. On the balcony stands a wet nurse holding a baby and a boy. They are admiring the procession of the troops, but the mother, covering her face with a handkerchief, has fallen back on the sofa, sobbing. Such also is the picture by Walter Langley, to which I have already referred, and such again is a picture by the French artist Morlon, depicting a lifeboat hastening in a heavy storm to the relief of a steamer that is being wrecked. Approaching these in kind are pictures which represent the hard-working peasant with respect and love. Such are the pictures by Millet, and particularly his drawing, "The Man with the Hoe"; also pictures in this style by Jules Breton, Lhermitte, Defregger, and others. As examples of pictures evoking indignation and horror at the violation of love of God and man, Gay's picture, "Judgment," may serve, and also Leizen-Mayer's, "Signing the Death Warrant." But there are also very few of this kind. Anxiety about the technique and the beauty of the picture for the most part obscures the feeling. For instance, Gérôme's "Pollice Verso" expresses not so much horror at what is being perpetrated as attraction by the beauty of the spectacle.[4]

To give examples from the modern art of our upper classes of art of the second kind, good universal art or even of the art of a whole people, is yet more difficult, especially in literary art and music. If there are some works which by their inner contents might be assigned to this class (such as *Don Quixote*, Molière's comedies, *David Copperfield* and *The Pickwick Papers* by Dickens, Gogol's and Pushkin's tales, and some things of Maupassant's), these works are for the most part—from the exceptional nature of the feelings they transmit, the superfluity of special details of time and locality, and, above all, on account of the poverty of their subject matter in comparison with examples of universal ancient art (such, for instance, as the story of Joseph)—comprehensible only to people of their own circle. That Joseph's brethren, being jealous of

4 In this picture the spectators in the Roman Amphitheater are turning down their thumbs to show that they wish the vanquished gladiator to be killed.—TR.

his father's affection, sell him to the merchants; that Potiphar's wife wishes to tempt the youth; that having attained
the highest station he takes pity on his brothers, including
Benjamin, the favorite—these and all the rest are feelings
accessible alike to a Russian peasant, a Chinese, an African,
a child, or an old man, educated or uneducated; and it is all
written with such restraint, is so free from any superfluous detail, that the story may be told to any circle and will be equally
comprehensible and touching to everyone. But not such are
the feelings of Don Quixote or of Molière's heroes (though
Molière is perhaps the most universal and therefore the most
excellent artist of modern times), nor of Pickwick and his
friends. These feelings are not common to all men, but very
exceptional; and therefore, to make them infectious, the
authors have surrounded them with abundant details of time
and place. And this abundance of detail makes the stories
difficult of comprehension to all people not living within reach
of the conditions described by the author.

The author of the novel of Joseph did not need to describe
in detail, as would be done nowadays, the blood-stained coat
of Joseph, the dwelling and dress of Jacob, the pose and attire
of Potiphar's wife, and how, adjusting the bracelet on her
left arm, she said, "Come to me," and so on, because the subject matter of feelings in this novel is so strong that all details
except the most essential—such as that Joseph went out into
another room to weep—are superfluous and would only hinder
the transmission of feelings. And therefore this novel is accessible to all men, touches people of all nations and classes,
young and old, and has lasted to our times, and will yet last
for thousands of years to come. But strip the best novels of
our times of their details and what will remain?

It is therefore impossible in modern literature to indicate
works fully satisfying the demands of universality. Such works
as exist are to a great extent spoiled by what is usually called
"realism," but would be better termed "provincialism," in art.

In music the same occurs as in verbal art, and for similar
reasons. In consequence of the poorness of the feeling they

contain, the melodies of the modern composers are amazingly empty and insignificant. And to strengthen the impression produced by these empty melodies, the new musicians pile complex modulations onto each trivial melody, not only in their own national manner but also in the way characteristic of their own exclusive circle and particular musical school. Melody—every melody—is free and may be understood by all men; but as soon as it is bound up with a particular harmony, it ceases to be accessible except to people trained to such harmony, and it becomes strange, not only to common men of another nationality, but to all who do not belong to the circle whose members have accustomed themselves to certain forms of harmonization. So music, like poetry, travels in a vicious circle. Trivial and exclusive melodies, in order to make them attractive, are laden with harmonic, rhythmic, and orchestral complications, and thus become yet more exclusive; and, far from being universal, are not even national, i.e., they are not comprehensible to the whole people but only to some people.

In music, besides marches and dances by various composers which satisfy the demands of universal art, one can indicate very few works of this class: Bach's famous violin aria, Chopin's nocturne in E-flat major, and perhaps a dozen bits (not whole pieces, but parts) selected from the works of Haydn, Mozart, Schubert, Beethoven, and Chopin.[5]

---

[5] While offering as examples of art those that seem to me the best, I attach no special importance to my selections; for, besides being insufficiently informed in all branches of art, I belong to the class of people whose taste has, by false training, been perverted. And therefore my old, inured habits may cause me to err, and I may mistake for absolute merit the impression a work produced on me in my youth. My only purpose in mentioning examples of works of this or that class is to make my meaning clearer, and to show how, with my present views, I understand excellence in art in relation to its subject matter. I must, moreover, mention that I consign my own artistic productions to the category of bad art, excepting the story "God sees the Truth," which seeks a place in the first class, and "The Prisoner of the Caucasus," which belongs to the second.

Although in painting the same thing is repeated as in poetry and music—namely, that in order to make them more interesting, works weak in conception are surrounded by minutely studied accessories of time and place which give them a temporary and local interest but make them less universal—still, in painting, more than in the other spheres of art, may be found works satisfying the demands of universal Christian art; that is to say, there are more works expressing feelings in which all men may participate.

In the arts of painting and sculpture all pictures and statues in so-called genre style, depictions of animals, landscapes and caricatures with subjects comprehensible to everyone, and also all kinds of ornaments, are universal in subject matter. Such productions in painting and sculpture are very numerous (e.g., china dolls), but for the most part such objects (for instance, ornaments of all kinds) are either not considered to be art or are considered to be art of a low quality. In reality all such objects, if only they transmit a true feeling experienced by the artist and comprehensible to everyone (however insignificant it may seem to us to be), are works of really good Christian art.

I fear it will here be urged against me that, having denied that the conception of beauty can supply a standard for works of art, I contradict myself by acknowledging ornaments to be works of good art. The reproach is unjust, for the subject matter of all kinds of ornamentation consists not in the beauty but in the feeling (of admiration of, and delight in, the combination of lines and colors) which the artist has experienced and with which he infects the spectator. Art remains what it was and what it must be: nothing but the infection by one man of another, or of others, with the feelings experienced by the infector. Among those feelings is the feeling of delight at what pleases the sight. Objects pleasing the sight may be such as please a small or a large number of people, or such as please all men. Ornaments for the most part are of the latter kind. A landscape representing a very unusual view, or a genre picture of a special subject, may not please everyone, but ornaments, from Yakutsk to the Greek, are intelligible to everyone and evoke a similar feeling of admiration in all, and therefore this despised kind of art should in Christian society be esteemed far above exceptional, pretentious pictures and sculptures.

So there are only two kinds of good Christian art; all the rest of art not comprised in these two divisions should be acknowledged to be bad art, deserving not to be encouraged but to be driven out, denied, and despised as being art which does not unite, but divides, people. Such, in literary art, are all novels and poems which transmit Church or patriotic feelings, and also exclusive feelings pertaining only to the class of the idle rich such as aristocratic honor, satiety, spleen, pessimism, and refined and vicious feelings flowing from sex-love—quite incomprehensible to the great majority of mankind.

In painting we must similarly place in the class of bad art all the Church, patriotic, and exclusive pictures; all the pictures representing the amusements and allurements of a rich and idle life; all the so-called symbolic pictures, in which the very meaning of the symbol is comprehensible only to the people of a certain circle; and, above all, pictures with voluptuous subjects—all that odious female nudity which fills all the exhibitions and galleries. And to this class belongs almost all the chamber and opera music of our times, beginning especially from Beethoven (Schumann, Berlioz, Liszt, Wagner), by its subject matter devoted to the expression of feelings accessible only to people who have developed in themselves an unhealthy, nervous irritation evoked by this exclusive, artificial, and complex music.

"What! the *Ninth Symphony* not a good work of art!" I hear exclaimed by indignant voices.

And I reply, Most certainly it is not. All that I have written I have written with the sole purpose of finding a clear and reasonable criterion by which to judge the merits of works of art. And this criterion, coinciding with the indications of plain and sane sense, indubitably shows me that that symphony by Beethoven is not a good work of art. Of course, to people educated in the adoration of certain productions and of their authors, to people whose taste has been perverted just by being educated in such adoration, the acknowledgment that such a celebrated work is bad is amazing and strange. But how are we to escape the indications of reason and of common sense?

Beethoven's *Ninth Symphony* is considered a great work of art. To verify its claim to be such, I must first ask myself whether this work transmits the highest religious feeling. I reply in the negative, for music in itself cannot transmit those feelings; and therefore I ask myself next, Since this work does not belong to the highest kind of religious art, has it the other characteristic of the good art of our time—the quality of uniting all men in one common feeling: does it rank as Christian universal art? And again I have no option but to reply in the negative; for not only do I not see how the feelings transmitted by this work could unite people not specially trained to submit themselves to its complex hypnotism, but I am unable to imagine to myself a crowd of normal people who could understand anything of this long, confused, and artificial production, except short snatches which are lost in a sea of what is incomprehensible. And therefore, whether I like it or not, I am compelled to conclude that this work belongs to the rank of bad art. It is curious to note in this connection that attached to the end of this very symphony is a poem of Schiller's which (though somewhat obscurely) expresses this very thought, namely, that feeling (Schiller speaks only of the feeling of gladness) unites people and evokes love in them. But though this poem is sung at the end of the symphony, the music does not accord with the thought expressed in the verses; for the music is exclusive and does not unite all men, but unites only a few, dividing them off from the rest of mankind.

And just in this same way, in all branches of art, many and many works considered great by the upper classes of our society will have to be judged. By this one sure criterion we shall have to judge the celebrated *Divine Comedy* and *Jerusalem Delivered,* and a great part of Shakespeare's and

Goethe's works, and in painting every representation of miracles, including Raphael's "Transfiguration," etc.

Whatever the work may be and however it may have been extolled, we have first to ask whether this work is one of real art or a counterfeit. Having acknowledged, on the basis of the indication of its infectiousness even to a small class of people, that a certain production belongs to the realm of art, it is necessary, on the basis of the indication of its accessibility, to decide the next question, Does this work belong to the category of bad, exclusive art, opposed to religious perception, or to Christian art uniting people? And having acknowledged an article to belong to real Christian art, we must then, according to whether it transmits the feelings flowing from love to God and man, or merely the simple feelings uniting all men, assign it a place in the ranks of religious art or in those of universal art.

Only on the basis of such verification shall we find it possible to select from the whole mass of what in our society claims to be art those works which form real, important, necessary spiritual food, and to separate them from all the harmful and useless art and from the counterfeits of art which surround us. Only on the basis of such verification shall we be able to rid ourselves of the pernicious results of harmful art and to avail ourselves of that beneficent action which is the purpose of true and good art and which is indispensable for the spiritual life of man and of humanity.

CHAPTER SEVENTEEN

A RT is one of two organs of human progress. By words man interchanges thoughts, by the forms of art he interchanges feelings, and this with all men, not only of the present time but also of the past and the future. It is natural to human beings to employ both these organs of intercommunication, and therefore the perversion of either of them must cause evil results to the society in which it occurs. And these results will be of two kinds: first, the absence in that society of the work which should be performed by the organ; and secondly, the harmful activity of the perverted organ. And just these results have shown themselves in our society. The organ of art has been perverted, and therefore the upper classes of society have to a great extent been deprived of the work that it should have performed. The diffusion in our society of enormous quantities of, on the one hand, those counterfeits of art which only serve to amuse and corrupt people, and, on the other hand, of works of insignificant, exclusive art, mistaken for the highest art, have perverted most men's capacity to be infected by true works of art, and have thus deprived them of the possibility of experiencing the highest feelings to which mankind has attained and which can only be transmitted from man to man by art.

All the best that has been done in art by man remains strange to people who lack the capacity to be infected by art, and is replaced either by spurious counterfeits of art or by insignificant art which they mistake for real art. People of our time and of our society are delighted with Baudelaires, Verlaines, Moréases, Ibsens, and Maeterlincks in poetry; with Monets, Manets, Puvis de Chavannes, Burne-Joneses, Stucks, and Böcklins in painting; with Wagners, Liszts, Richard Strausses, in music; and they are no longer capable of comprehending either the highest or the simplest art.

In the upper classes, in consequence of this loss of capacity to be infected by works of art, people grow up, are educated, and live, lacking the fertilizing, improving influence of art, and therefore not only do not advance toward perfection, do not become kinder, but, on the contrary, possessing highly developed external means of civilization, they yet tend to become continually more savage, more coarse, and more cruel.

Such is the result of the absence from our society of the activity of that essential organ—art. But the consequences of the perverted activity of that organ are yet more harmful. And they are numerous.

The first consequence, plain for all to see, is the enormous expenditure of the labor of working people on things which are not only useless, but which, for the most part, are harmful; and more than that, the waste of priceless human lives on this unnecessary and harmful business. It is terrible to consider with what intensity, and amid what privations, millions of people—who lack time and opportunity to attend to what they and their families urgently require—labor for ten, twelve, or fourteen hours on end, and even at night, setting the type for pseudo-artistic books which spread vice among mankind, or working for theaters, concerts, exhibitions, and picture galleries, which, for the most part, also serve vice; but it is yet more terrible to reflect that lively, kindly children, capable of all that is good, are devoted from their early years to such tasks as these: that for six, eight, or ten hours a day, and for ten or fifteen years, some of them should play scales and exercises; others should twist their limbs, walk on their toes, and lift their legs above their heads; a third set should sing solfeggios; a fourth set, showing themselves off in all manner of ways, should pronounce verses; a fifth set should draw from busts or from nude models and paint studies; a sixth set should write compositions according to the rules of certain periods; and that in these occupations, unworthy of a human being, which are often continued long after full maturity, they should waste their physical and mental strength and lose all perception of the meaning of life. It is often said that it is horrible and pitiful to see little acrobats putting their legs over their necks, but it is not less pitiful to see children of ten giving concerts, and it is still worse to see schoolboys of ten who, as a preparation for literary work, have learned by heart the exceptions to the Latin grammar. These people not only grow physically and mentally deformed, but also morally deformed and become incapable of doing anything really needed by man. Occupying in society the role of amusers of the rich, they lose their sense of human dignity and develop in themselves such a passion for public applause that they are always a prey to an inflated and unsatisfied vanity which grows in them to diseased dimensions, and they expend their mental strength in efforts to obtain satisfaction for this passion. And what is most tragic of all is that these people, who for the sake of art are spoiled for life, not only do not render service to this art, but, on the contrary, inflict the greatest harm on it. They are taught in academies, schools, and conservatories how to counterfeit art, and by learning this they so pervert themselves that they quite lose the capacity to produce works of real art, and become purveyors of that counterfeit, or trivial, or depraved art which floods our society. This is the first obvious consequence of the perversion of the organ of art.

The second consequence is that the productions of amusement-art, which are prepared in such terrific quantities by the armies of professional artists, enable the rich people of our times to live the lives they do, lives not only unnatural, but in contradiction to the humane principles these people themselves profess. To live as do the rich, idle people, especially the women, far from nature and from animals, in artificial conditions, with muscles atrophied or misdeveloped by gymnastics, and with enfeebled vital energy, would be impossible were it not for what is called art—for this occupation and amusement which hides from them the meaninglessness of their lives and saves them from the dullness that oppresses them. Take from all these people the theaters, concerts, exhibitions, piano playing, songs, and novels with which they now fill their time, in full confidence that occupation with these things is a very refined, aesthetical, and therefore good occupation; take from the patrons of art who buy pictures, assist musicians, and are acquainted with writers, their role of protectors of that important matter "art," and they will not be able to continue such a life but will all be eaten up by ennui and spleen, and will become conscious of the meaninglessness and wrongness of their present mode of life. Only occupation with what, among them, is considered art renders it possible for them to continue to live on, infringing all natural conditions without perceiving the emptiness and cruelty of their lives. And this support afforded to the false manner of life pursued by the rich is the second consequence, and a serious one, of the perversion of art.

The third consequence of the perversion of art is the perplexity produced in the minds of children and of plain folk. Among people not perverted by the false theories of our society, among workers and children, there exists a very definite conception of what people may be respected and praised for. In the minds of peasants and children the ground for praise or eulogy can only be either physical strength (Hercules, the heroes and conquerors) or moral, spiritual, strength (Sakya Muni giving up a beautiful wife and a kingdom to save mankind, Christ going to the cross for the truth he professed, and all the martyrs and the saints). Both are understood by peasants and children. They understand that physical strength must be respected, for it compels respect; and the moral strength of goodness an unperverted man cannot fail to respect because all his spiritual being draws him toward it. But these people, children and peasants, suddenly perceive that besides those praised, respected, and rewarded for physical or moral strength, there are others who are praised, extolled, and rewarded much more than the heroes of strength and virtue merely because they sing well, compose verses, or dance. They see that singers, composers, painters, ballet dancers earn millions of rubles and receive more honor than the saints do; and peasants and children are perplexed.

When fifty years had elapsed after Pushkin's death, and, simultaneously, the cheap edition of his works began to circulate among the people and a monument was erected to him in Moscow, I received more than a dozen letters from different peasants asking why Pushkin was raised to such dignity. And only the other day a literate man from Sarato [1] called on me

1 In Russian it is customary to make a distinction between literate and illiterate people, i.e., between those who can and those who cannot read. *Literate* in this sense does not imply that the man would speak or write correctly.—TR.

who had evidently gone out of his mind over this very question. He was on his way to Moscow to expose the clergy for having taken part in raising a "monament" to Mr. Pushkin.

Indeed, one need only imagine to oneself what the state of mind of such a man of the people must be when he learns from such rumors and newspapers as reach him that the clergy, the Government officials, and all the best people in Russia are triumphantly unveiling a statue to a great man, the benefactor, the pride of Russia—Pushkin, of whom till then he had never heard. From all sides he reads or hears about this, and he naturally supposes that if such honors are rendered to anyone, then without doubt he must have done something extraordinary—either some feat of strength or of goodness. He tries to learn who Pushkin was, and having discovered that Pushkin was neither a hero nor a general, but was a private person and a writer, he comes to the conclusion that Pushkin must have been a holy man and a teacher of goodness, and he hastens to read or to hear his life and works. But what must be his perplexity when he learns that Pushkin was a man of more than easy morals, who was killed in a duel, i.e., when attempting to murder another man, and that all his service consisted in writing verses about love, which were often very indecent.

That a hero, or Alexander the Great, or Genghis Khan, or Napoleon were great, he understands because any one of them could have crushed him and a thousand like him; that Buddha, Socrates, and Christ were great he also understands, for he knows and feels that he and all men should be such as they were; but why a man should be great because he wrote verses about the love of women he cannot make out.

A similar perplexity must trouble the brain of a Breton or Norman peasant who hears that a monument, *une statue* (as to the Madonna), is being erected to Baudelaire, and reads, or is told, what the contents of his *Fleurs du Mal* are; or, more amazing still, to Verlaine, when he learns the story of that man's wretched, vicious life, and reads his verses. And what confusion it must cause in the brains of peasants when they learn that some Patti or Taglioni is paid $50,000 for a season, or that a painter gets as much for a picture, or that authors of novels describing love scenes have received even more than that.

And it is the same with children. I remember how I passed through this stage of amazement and stupefaction, and only reconciled myself to this exaltation of artists to the level of heroes and saints by lowering in my own estimation the importance of moral excellence, and by attributing a false, unnatural meaning to works of art. And a similar confusion must occur in the soul of each child and each man of the people when he learns of the strange honors and rewards that are lavished on artists. This is the third consequence of the false relation in which our society stands toward art.

The fourth consequence is that people of the upper classes, more and more frequently encountering the contradictions between beauty and goodness, put the ideal of beauty first, thus freeing themselves from the demands of morality. These people, reversing the roles, instead of admitting, as is really the case, that the art they serve is an antiquated affair, allege that morality is an antiquated affair which can have no importance for people situated on that high plane of development on which they opine that they are situated.

This result of the false relation to art showed itself in our society long ago; but recently, with its prophet Nietzsche and his adherents and with the Decadents and certain English aesthetes who coincide with him, it is being expressed with especial impudence. The Decadents and aesthetes of the type at one time represented by Oscar Wilde select as a theme for their productions the denial of morality and the laudation of vice.

This art has partly generated, and partly coincides with, a similar philosophic theory. I recently received from America a book entitled *The Survival of the Fittest: Philosophy of Power* by Ragnar Redbeard (Chicago, 1896). The substance of

this book, as it is expressed in the editor's preface, is that to
measure "right" by the false philosophy of the Hebrew
prophets and "weepful" Messiahs is madness. Right is not the
offspring of doctrine, but of power. All laws, commandments,
or doctrines as to not doing to another what you do not wish
done to you have no inherent authority whatever, but receive
it only from the club, the gallows, and the sword. A man truly
free is under no obligation to obey any injunction, human or
divine. Obedience is the sign of the degenerate. Disobedience
is the stamp of the hero. Men should not be bound by moral
rules invented by their foes. The whole world is a slippery
battlefield. Ideal justice demands that the vanquished should
be exploited, emasculated, and scorned. The free and brave
may seize the world. And, therefore, there should be eternal
war for life, for land, for love, for women, for power, and for
gold. (Something similar was said a few years ago by the
celebrated and refined academician, Vogüé.) The earth and its
treasures is "booty for the bold."

The author has evidently by himself, independently of
Nietzsche, come to the same conclusions which are professed
by the new artists.

Expressed in the form of a doctrine these positions startle
us. In reality they are implied in the ideal of art serving
beauty. The art of our upper classes has educated people in
this ideal of the superman,[2]—which is, in reality, the old ideal
of Nero, Stenka Razin,[3] Genghis Khan, Robert Macaire,[4] or

[2] The superman (Übermensch), in the Nietzschean philosophy, is that
superior type of man whom the struggle for existence is to evolve, and
who will seek only his own power and pleasure, will know nothing of
pity and will have the right, because he will possess the power, to make
ordinary people serve him.—TR.

[3] Stenka Razin was by origin a common Cossack. His brother was hung
for a breach of military discipline, and to this event Stenka Razin's hatred
of the governing classes has been attributed. He formed a robber band
and subsequently headed a formidable rebellion, declaring himself in
favor of freedom for the serfs, religious toleration, and the abolition of
taxes. Like the government he opposed, he relied on force, and, though

Napoleon, and all their accomplices, assistants, and adulators
—and it supports this ideal with all its might.

It is this supplanting of the ideal of what is right by the
ideal of what is beautiful, i.e., of what is pleasant, that is the
fourth consequence, and a terrible one, of the perversion of
art in our society. It is fearful to think of what would befall
humanity were such art to spread among the masses of the
people. And it already begins to spread.

Finally, the fifth and chief result is that the art which
flourishes in the upper classes of European society has a
directly vitiating influence, infecting people with the worst
feelings and with those most harmful to humanity—superstition, patriotism, and, above all, sensuality.

Look carefully into the causes of the ignorance of the
masses, and you may see that the chief cause does not at all
lie in the lack of schools and libraries as we are accustomed
to suppose, but in those superstitions, both ecclesiastical and
patriotic, with which the people are saturated and which are
unceasingly generated by all the methods of art. Church
superstitions are supported and produced by the poetry of
prayers, hymns, painting, by the sculpture of images and of
statues, by singing, by organs, by music, by architecture, and
even by dramatic art in religious ceremonies. Patriotic superstitions are supported and produced by verses and stories
which are supplied even in schools, by music, by songs, by
triumphal processions, by royal meetings, by martial pictures,
and by monuments.

Were it not for this continual activity in all departments of
art, perpetuating the ecclesiastical and patriotic intoxication

---

he used it largely in defense of the poor against the rich, he still held to

"The good old rule, the simple plan,
That they should take who have the power,
And they should keep who can."

Like Robin Hood, he is favorably treated in popular legends.—Tr.

4 Robert Macaire is a modern type of adroit and audacious rascality.
He was the hero of a popular play produced in Paris in 1834.—Tr.

and embitterment of the people, the masses would long before this have attained to true enlightenment.

But it is not only in Church matters and patriotic matters that art depraves; it is art in our time that serves as the chief cause of the perversion of people in the most important question of social life—in their sexual relations. We nearly all know by our own experience, and those who are fathers and mothers know in the case of their grown-up children also, what fearful mental and physical suffering, what useless waste of strength, people suffer merely as a consequence of dissoluteness in sexual desire.

Since the world began, since the Trojan war, which sprang from that same sexual dissoluteness, down to and including the suicides and murders of lovers described in almost every newspaper, a great proportion of the sufferings of the human race have come from this source.

And what is art doing? All art, real and counterfeit, with very few exceptions is devoted to describing, depicting, and inflaming sexual love in every shape and form. When one remembers all those novels and their lust-kindling descriptions of love, from the most refined to the grossest, with which the literature of our society overflows; if one only remembers all those pictures and statues representing women's naked bodies, and all sorts of abominations which are reproduced in illustrations and advertisements; if one only remembers all the filthy operas and operettas, songs, and romances with which our world teems, involuntarily it seems as if existing art had but one definite aim—to disseminate vice as widely as possible.

Such, though not all, are the most direct consequences of that perversion of art which has occurred in our society. So that what in our society is called art not only does not conduce to the progress of mankind, but more than almost anything else hinders the attainment of goodness in our lives.

And therefore the question which involuntarily presents itself to every man free from artistic activity and therefore not bound to existing art by self-interest, the question asked by me at the beginning of this work, "Is it just that to what we call art, to a something belonging to but a small section of society, should be offered up such sacrifices of human labor, of human lives, and of goodness as are now being offered up?" receives the natural reply, "No; it is unjust, and these things should not be!" This is also the answer of sound sense and unperverted moral feeling. Not only should these things not be, not only should no sacrifices be offered up to what among us is called art, but, on the contrary, the efforts of those who wish to live rightly should be directed toward the destruction of this art, for it is one of the most cruel of the evils that harass our section of humanity. So that, were the question put, "Would it be preferable for our Christian world to be deprived of *all* that is now esteemed to be art, and together with the false lose *all* that is good in it?" I think that every reasonable and moral man would again decide the question as Plato decided it for his *Republic* and as all the Church Christian and Mo hammedan teachers of mankind decided it, i.e., would say "Rather let there be no art at all than continue the deprav ing art, or simulation of art, which now exists." Happily, nc one has to face this question, and no one need adopt eithei solution. All that man can do and that we—the so-called edu cated people, who are so placed that we have the possibility of understanding the meaning of the phenomena of our life —can and should do is to understand the error we are involved in, and not harden our hearts in it but seek for a way of escape.

CHAPTER EIGHTEEN

THE cause of the lie into which the art of our society has fallen was that people of the upper classes, having ceased to believe in the Church teaching (called Christian), did not resolve to accept true Christian teaching in its real and fundamental principles of sonship to God and brotherhood to man, but continued to live on without any belief, endeavoring to make up for the absence of belief—some by hypocrisy, pretending still to believe in the nonsense of the Church creeds; others by boldly asserting their disbelief; others by refined agnosticism; and others, again, by returning to the Greek worship of beauty, proclaiming egotism to be right and elevating it to the rank of a religious doctrine.

The cause of the malady was the non-acceptance of Christ's teaching in its real, i.e., its full meaning. And the only cure for the illness lies in acknowledging that teaching in its full meaning. And such acknowledgment in our time is not only possible, but inevitable. Already today a man standing on the height of the knowledge of our age, whether he be nominally a Catholic or a Protestant, cannot say that he really believes in the dogmas of the Church: in God being a Trinity, in Christ being God, in the scheme of redemption, and so forth; nor can he satisfy himself by proclaiming his unbelief or skepticism, nor by relapsing into the worship of beauty and egotism. Above all, he can no longer say that we do not know the real meaning of Christ's teaching. That meaning has not only become accessible to all men of our times, but the whole life of man today is permeated by the spirit of that teaching, and, consciously or unconsciously, is guided by it.

However differently in form people belonging to our Christian world may define the destiny of man, whether they see it in human progress in whatever sense of the words, in the union of all men in a socialistic realm, or in the establishment of a commune, whether they look forward to the union of mankind under the guidance of one universal Church, or to the federation of the world—however various in form their definitions of the destination of human life may be, all men in our times already admit that the highest well-being attainable by men is to be reached by their union with one another.

However people of our upper classes (feeling that their ascendancy can only be maintained as long as they separate themselves—the rich and learned—from the laborers, the poor and the unlearned) may seek to devise new conceptions of life by which their privileges may be perpetuated—now the ideal of returning to antiquity, now mysticism, now Hellenism, now the cult of the superior person (supermanism)—they have, willingly or unwillingly, to admit the truth which is elucidating itself from all sides, voluntarily and involuntarily, namely, that our welfare lies only in the unification and the brotherhood of man.

Unconsciously this truth is confirmed by the construction of means of communication, telegraphs, telephones, the press, and the ever increasing attainability of material well-being for everyone; consciously it is affirmed by the destruction of superstitions which divide men, by the diffusion of the truths of knowledge, and by the expression of the ideal of the brotherhood of man in the best works of art of our time.

Art is a spiritual organ of human life which cannot be destroyed, and therefore, notwithstanding all the efforts made by people of the upper classes to conceal the religious ideal by which humanity lives, that.ideal is more and more clearly recognized by man, and even in our perverted society is more and more often partially expressed by science and by art. During the present century works of the higher kind of religious art have appeared more and more frequently, both in literature and in painting, permeated by a truly Christian spirit, as also works of the universal art of common life accessible to all. So that even art knows the true ideal of our times and tends toward it. On the one hand, the best works of art of our times transmit religious feelings urging toward the union and the brotherhood of man (such are the works of Dickens, Hugo, Dostoevsky, and in painting of Millet, Bastien Lepage, Jules Breton, Lhermitte, and others); on the other hand, they strive toward the transmission, not of feelings which are natural to people of the upper classes only, but of such feelings as may unite everyone without exception. There are as yet few such works, but the need of them is already acknowledged. In recent times we also meet more and more frequently with attempts at publications, pictures, concerts, and theaters for the people. All this is still very far from accomplishing what should be done, but already the direction in which good art instinctively presses forward to regain the path natural to it can be discerned.

The religious perception of our time—which consists in acknowledging that the aim of life (both collective and individual) is the union of mankind—is already so sufficiently distinct that people have now only to reject the false theory of beauty according to which enjoyment is considered to be the purpose of art, and religious perception will naturally take its place as the guide of the art of our time.

And as soon as the religious perception, which already unconsciously directs the life of man, is consciously acknowledged, then immediately and naturally the division of art into art for the lower and art for the upper classes will disappear. There will be one common, brotherly, universal art, and first that art will naturally be rejected which transmits feelings incompatible with the religious perception of our time, feelings which do not unite, but divide men, and then that insignificant, exclusive art will be rejected to which an importance is now attached to which it has no right.

And as soon as this occurs, art will immediately cease to be what it has been in recent times, a means of making people coarser and more vicious, and it will become what it always used to be and should be, a means by which humanity progresses toward unity and blessedness.

Strange as the comparison may sound, what has happened to the art of our circle and time is what happens to a woman who sells her womanly attractiveness, intended for maternity, for the pleasure of those who desire such pleasures.

The art of our time and of our circle has become a prostitute. And this comparison holds good even in minute details. Like her it is not limited to certain times, like her it is always adorned, like her it is always salable, and like her it is enticing and ruinous.

A real work of art can only arise in the soul of an artist occasionally as the fruit of the life he has lived, just as a child is conceived by its mother. But counterfeit art is produced by artisans and handicraftsmen continually, if only consumers can be found.

Real art, like the wife of an affectionate husband, needs no ornaments. But counterfeit art, like a prostitute, must always be decked out.

The cause of the production of real art is the artist's inner need to express a feeling that has accumulated, just as for a mother the cause of sexual conception is love. The cause of counterfeit art, as of prostitution, is gain.

The consequence of true art is the introduction of a new feeling into the intercourse of life, as the consequence of a wife's love is the birth of a new man into life.

The consequences of counterfeit art are the perversion of man, pleasure which never satisfies, and the weakening of man's spiritual strength.

And this is what people of our day and of our circle should understand in order to avoid the filthy torrent of depraved and prostituted art with which we are deluged.

CHAPTER NINETEEN

PEOPLE talk of the art of the future, meaning by "art of the future" some especially refined, new art, which, as they imagine, will be developed out of that exclusive art of one class which is now considered the highest art. But no such new art of the future can or will be found. Our exclusive art, that of the upper classes of Christendom, has found its way into a blind alley. The direction in which it has been going leads nowhere. Having once let go of that which is most essential for art (namely, the guidance given by religious perception), that art has become ever more and more exclusive and therefore ever more and more perverted, until finally it has come to nothing. The art of the future, that which is really coming, will not be a development of present-day art but will

arise on completely other and new foundations, having nothing in common with those by which our present art of the
upper classes is guided.

Art of the future, that is to say, such part of art as will be
chosen from among all the art diffused among mankind, will
consist not in transmitting feelings accessible only to members
of the rich classes, as is the case today, but in transmitting
such feelings as embody the highest religious perception of
our times. Only those productions will be considered art
which transmit feelings drawing men together in brotherly
union, or such universal feelings as can unite all men. Only
such art will be chosen, tolerated, approved, and diffused. But
art transmitting feelings flowing from antiquated, worn-out
religious teaching—Church art, patriotic art, voluptuous art,
transmitting feelings of superstitious fear, of pride, of vanity,
of ecstatic admiration of national heroes—art exciting either
exclusive love of one's own people or sensuality—will be considered bad, harmful art and will be censured and despised
by public opinion. All the rest of art, transmitting feelings
accessible only to a section of people, will be considered unimportant and will be neither blamed nor praised. And the appraisement of art in general will devolve, not, as is now the
case, on a separate class of rich people, but on the whole people; so that for a work to be esteemed good and to be approved of and diffused, it will have to satisfy the demands, not
of a few people living in identical and often unnatural conditions, but it will have to satisfy the demands of all those great
masses of people who are situated in the natural conditions
of laborious life.

And the artists producing art will also not be, as now,
merely a few people selected from a small section of the nation, members of the upper classes or their hangers-on, but
will consist of all those gifted members of the whole people
who prove capable of, and are inclined toward, artistic activity.

Artistic activity will then be accessible to all men. It will
become accessible to the whole people because, in the first

place, in the art of the future not only will that complex technique which deforms the productions of the art of today and requires so great an effort and expenditure of time not be demanded, but, on the contrary, the demand will be for clearness, simplicity, and brevity—conditions mastered not by mechanical exercises but by the education of taste. And secondly, artistic activity will become accessible to all men of the people because, instead of the present professional schools which only some can enter, all will learn music and depictive art (singing and drawing) equally with letters in the elementary schools, and in such a way that every man, having received the first principles of drawing and music and feeling a capacity for, and a call to, one or other of the arts, will be able to perfect himself in it.

People think that if there are no special art schools the technique of art will deteriorate. Undoubtedly, if by technique we understand those complications of art which are now considered an excellence, it will deteriorate; but if by technique is understood clearness, beauty, simplicity, and compression in works of art, then, even if the elements of drawing and music were not to be taught in the national schools, the technique will not only not deteriorate but, as is shown by all peasant art, will be a hundred times better. It will be improved, because all the artists of genius now hidden among the masses will become producers of art and will give models of excellence, which (as has always been the case) will be the best schools of technique for their successors. For every true artist even now learns his technique chiefly not in the schools, but in life, from the examples of the great masters; then—when the producers of art will be the best artists of the whole nation, and there will be more such examples, and they will be more accessible—such part of the school training as the future artist will lose will be a hundredfold compensated for by the training he will receive from the numerous examples of good art diffused in society.

Such will be one difference between present and future art. Another difference will be that art will not be produced by

professional artists receiving payment for their work and engaged on nothing else besides their art. The art of the future
will be produced by all the members of the community who
feel the need of such activity, but they will occupy themselves
with art only when they feel such need.

In our society people think that an artist will work better
and produce more if he has a secured maintenance. And this
opinion would serve once more to show clearly, were such
demonstration still needed, that what among us is considered
art is not art but only its counterfeit. It is quite true that
for the producion of boots or loaves division of labor is very
advantageous, and that the bootmaker or baker who need not
prepare his own dinner or fetch his own fuel will make more
boots or loaves than if he had to busy himself about these
matters. But art is not a handicraft; it is the transmission of
feeling the artist has experienced. And sound feeling can only
be engendered in a man when he is living on all its sides the
life natural and proper to mankind. And therefore security of
maintenance is a condition most harmful to an artist's true
productiveness since it removes him from the condition natural to all men—that of struggle with nature for the maintenance of both his own life and that of others—and thus de-
prives him of opportunity and possibility to experience the
most important and natural feelings of man. There is no position more injurious to an artist's productiveness than that position of complete security and luxury in which artists usually
live in our society.

The artist of the future will live the common live of man,
earning his subsistence by some kind of labor. The fruits of
that highest spiritual strength which passes through him he
will try to share with the greatest possible number of people,
for in such transmission to others of the feelings that have
arisen in him he will find his happiness and his reward. The
artist of the future will be unable to understand how an artist, whose chief delight is in the wide diffusion of his works,
could give them only in exchange for a certain payment.

Until the dealers are driven out, the temple of art will not be a temple. But the art of the future will drive them out.

And therefore the subject matter of the art of the future, as I imagine it to myself, will be totally unlike that of today. It will consist not in the expression of exclusive feelings of pride, spleen, satiety, and all possible forms of voluptuousness, available and interesting only to people who by force have freed themselves from the labor natural to human beings; but it will consist in the expression of feelings experienced by a man living the life natural to all men and flowing from the religious perception of our times, or of such feelings as are open to all men without exception.

To people of our circle who do not know and cannot or will not understand the feelings which will form the subject matter of the art of the future, such subject matter appears very poor in comparison with those subtleties of exclusive art with which they are now occupied. "What is there fresh to be said in the sphere of the Christian feeling of love of one's fellow man? The feelings common to everyone are so insignificant and monotonous," think they. And yet, in our time, the really fresh feelings can only be religious, Christian feelings, and such as are open, accessible to all. The feelings flowing from the religious perception of our times, Christian feelings, are infinitely new and varied, only not in the sense some people imagine—not that they can be evoked by the depiction of Christ and of gospel episodes, or by repeating in new forms the Christian truths of unity, brotherhood, equality, and love —but in that all the oldest, commonest, and most hackneyed phenomena of life evoke the newest, most unexpected, and touching emotions as soon as a man regards them from the Christian point of view.

What can be older than the relations between married couples, of parents to children, of children to parents; the relations of men to their fellow countrymen and to foreigners, to an invasion, to defense, to property, to the land, or to animals? But as soon as a man regards these matters from the

Christian point of view, endlessly varied, fresh, complex, and strong emotions immediately arise.

And, in the same way, that realm of subject matter for the art of the future which relates to the simplest feelings of common life open to all will not be narrowed but widened. In our former art only the expression of feelings natural to people of a certain exceptional position was considered worthy of being transmitted by art, and even then only on condition that these feelings were transmitted in a most refined manner, incomprehensible to the majority of men; all the immense realm of folk art and children's art—jests, proverbs, riddles, songs, dances, children's games, and mimicry—was not esteemed a domain worthy of art.

The artist of the future will understand that to compose a fairy tale, a little song which will touch, a lullaby or a riddle which will entertain, a jest which will amuse, or to draw a sketch which will delight dozens of generations or millions of children and adults, is incomparably more important and more fruitful than to compose a novel or a symphony, or paint a picture which will divert some members of the wealthy classes for a short time, and then be forever forgotten. The region of this art of the simple feelings accessible to all is enormous, and it is as yet almost untouched.

The art of the future, therefore, will not be poorer, but infinitely richer in subject matter. And the form of the art of the future will also not be inferior to the present forms of art, but infinitely superior to them. Superior, not in the sense of having a refined and complex technique, but in the sense of the capacity briefly, simply, and clearly to transmit, without any superfluities, the feeling which the artist has experienced and wishes to transmit.

I remember once speaking to a famous astronomer who had given public lectures on the spectrum analysis of the stars of the Milky Way, and saying it would be a good thing if with his knowledge and masterly delivery he would give a lecture merely on the formation and movements of the earth, for certainly there were many people at his lecture on the spectrum analysis of the stars of the Milky Way, especially among the women, who did not well know why night follows day and summer follows winter. The wise astronomer smiled as he answered, "Yes, it would be a good thing, but it would be very difficult. To lecture on the spectrum analysis of the Milky Way is far easier."

And so it is in art. To write a rhymed poem dealing with the times of Cleopatra, or paint a picture of Nero burning Rome, or compose a symphony in the manner of Brahms or Richard Strauss, or an opera like Wagner's, is far easier than to tell a simple story without any unnecessary details, yet so that it should transmit the feelings of the narrator, or to draw a pencil sketch which should touch or amuse the beholder, or to compose four bars of clear and simple melody, without any accompaniment, which should convey an impression and be remembered by those who hear it.

"It is impossible for us, with our culture, to return to a primitive state," say the artists of our time. "It is impossible for us now to write such stories as that of Joseph or the *Odyssey,* to produce such statues as the Venus of Milo, or to compose such music as the folk songs."

And indeed, for the artists of our society and day it is impossible, but not for the future artist who will be free from all the perversion of technical improvements hiding the absence of subject matter, and who, not being a professional artist and receiving no payment for his activity, will only produce art when he feels impelled to do so by an irresistible inner impulse.

The art of the future will thus be completely distinct, both in subject matter and in form, from what is now called art. The only subject matter of the art of the future will be either feelings drawing men toward union, or such as already unite them; and the forms of art will be such as will be open to everyone. And therefore, the ideal of excellence in the future will not be the exclusiveness of feeling, accessible only to some, but, on the contrary, its universality. And not bulkiness, obscurity, and complexity of form, as is now esteemed, but, on the contrary, brevity, clearness, and simplicity of expression. Only when art has attained to that, will art neither divert nor deprave men as it does now, calling on them to expend their best strength on it, but be what it should be—a vehicle wherewith to transmit religious, Christian perception from the realm of reason and intellect into that of feeling, and really drawing people in actual life nearer to that perfection and unity indicated to them by their religious perception.

CHAPTER TWENTY

THE CONCLUSION

I HAVE accomplished, to the best of my ability, this work which has occupied me for fifteen years on a subject near to me—that of art. By saying that this subject has occupied me for fifteen years, I do not mean that I have been writing this book fifteen years, but only that I began to write on art fifteen years ago, thinking that when once I undertook the task I should be able to accomplish it without a break. It proved, however, that my views on the matter then were so far from clear that I could not arrange them in a way that satisfied me. From that time I have never ceased to think on the subject, and I have started to write on it six or seven times, but each time, after writing a considerable part of it, I have found myself unable to bring the work to a satisfactory conclusion, and have had to put it aside. Now I have finished it; and however badly I may have performed the task, my hope is that my fundamental thought as to the false direction the art of our society has taken and is following, as to the reasons of this, and as to the real destination of art, is correct and that therefore my work will not be without avail. But that this should come to pass and that art should really abandon its false path and take the new direction, it is necessary that another equally important human spiritual activity—science—in intimate dependence on which art always rests, should abandon the false path which it too, like art, is following.

Science and art are as closely bound together as the lungs and heart, so that if one organ is vitiated the other cannot act rightly.

True science investigates and brings to human perception such truths and such knowledge as the people of a given time and society consider most important. Art transmits these truths from the region of perception to the region of emotion. Therefore, if the path chosen by science be false, so also will be the path taken by art. Science and art are like a certain kind of barge with kedge-anchors which used to ply on our rivers. Science, like the boats which took the anchors upstream and made them secure, gives direction to the forward movement, while art, like the windlass worked on the barge to draw it toward the anchor, causes the actual progression. And thus a false activity of science inevitably causes a correspondingly false activity of art.

As art in general is the transmission of every kind of feeling, but in the limited sense of the word we only call art that which transmits feelings acknowledged by us to be important, so also science in general is the transmission of all possible knowledge; but in the limited sense of the word we call science that which transmits knowledge acknowledged by us to be important.

And the degree of importance, both of the feelings transmitted by art and of the information transmitted by science, is decided by the religious perception of the given time and society, i.e., by the common understanding of the purpose of their lives possessed by the people of that time or society.

That which most of all contributes to the fulfilment of that purpose will be studied most; that which contributes less will be studied less; that which does not contribute at all to the fulfilment of the purpose of human life will be entirely neglected, or, if studied, such study will not be accounted science. So it always has been, and so it should be now, for such is the nature of human knowledge and of human life. But the sci-

ence of the upper classes of our time, which not only does not
acknowledge any religion, but considers every religion to be
mere superstition, could not and cannot make such distinc-
tions.

Scientists of our day affirm that they study *everything* impartially; but as everything is too much (is in fact an infinite
number of objects), and as it is impossible to study all alike,
this is only said in theory, while in practice not everything is
studied and study is applied far from impartially, only that
being studied which, on the one hand, is most wanted by, and,
on the other hand, is pleasantest to, those people who occupy
themselves with science. And what the people belonging to
the upper classes who are occupying themselves with science
most want is the maintenance of the system under which those
classes retain their privileges; and what is pleasantest are such
things as satisfy idle curiosity, do not demand great mental
efforts, and can be practically applied.

And therefore one side of science, including theology and
philosophy adapted to the existing order, as also history and
political economy of the same sort, is chiefly occupied in
proving that the existing order is the very one which ought to
exist, that it has come into existence and continues to exist
by the operation of immutable laws not amenable to human
will, and that all efforts to change it are therefore harmful
and wrong. The other part, experimental science—including
mathematics, astronomy, chemistry, physics, botany, and all
the natural sciences—is exclusively occupied with things that
have no direct relation to human life: with what is curious
and with things of which practical application advantageous
to people of the upper classes can be made. And to justify
that selection of objects of study which (in conformity to
their own position) the men of science of our times have
made, they have devised a theory of science for science's sake,
quite similar to the theory of art for art's sake.

As by the theory of art for art's sake it appears that occupation with all those things that please us is art, so, by the

theory of science for science's sake, the study of that which interests us is science.

So that one side of science, instead of studying how people should live in order to fulfil their mission in life, demonstrates the righteousness and immutability of the bad and false arrangements of life which exist around us, while the other part, experimental science, occupies itself with questions of simple curiosity or with technical improvements.

The first of these divisions of science is harmful, not only because it confuses people's perceptions and gives false decisions, but also because it exists and occupies the ground which should belong to true science. It does this harm, that each man, in order to approach the study of the most important questions of life, must first refute these erections of lies which have during ages been piled around each of the most essential questions of human life and which are propped up by all the strength of human ingenuity.

The second division—the one of which modern science is so particularly proud and which is considered by many people to be the only real science—is harmful in that it diverts attention from the really important subjects to insignificant subjects, and is also directly harmful in that, under the evil system of society which the first division of science justifies and supports, a great part of the technical gains of science are turned not to the advantage but to the injury of mankind.

Indeed, it is only to those who are devoting their lives to such study that it seems as if all the inventions which are made in the sphere of natural science were very important and useful things. And to these people it seems so only when they do not look around them and do not see what is really important. They only need tear themselves away from the psychological microscope under which they examine the objects of their study and look about them in order to see how insignificant is all that has afforded them such naïve pride, all that knowledge not only of geometry of n-dimensions, spectrum analysis of the Milky Way, the form of atoms, dimensions of human skulls of the Stone Age, and similar trifles, but even our knowledge of micro-organisms, X-rays, etc., in comparison with such knowledge as we have thrown aside and handed over to the perversions of the professors of theology, jurisprudence, political economy, financial science, etc. We need only look around us to perceive that the activity proper to real science is not the study of whatever happens to interest us, but the study of how man's life should be established—the study of those questions of religion, morality, and social life, without the solution of which all our knowledge of nature will be harmful or insignificant.

We are highly delighted and very proud that our science renders it possible to utilize the energy of a waterfall and make it work in factories, or that we have pierced tunnels through mountains, and so forth. But the pity of it is that we make the force of the waterfall labor, not for the benefit of the workmen, but to enrich capitalists who produce articles of luxury or weapons of man-destroying war. The same dynamite with which we blast the mountains to pierce tunnels we use for the wars from which we not only do not intend to abstain, but which we consider inevitable and for which we unceasingly prepare.

If we are now able to inoculate preventively with diphtheritic microbes, to find a needle in a body by means of X-rays, to straighten a hunchback, cure syphilis, and perform wonderful operations, we should not be proud of these acquisitions either (even were they all established beyond dispute) if we fully understood the true purpose of real science. If but one-tenth of the efforts now spent on objects of pure curiosity or of merely practical application were expended on real science organizing the life of man, more than half the people now sick would not have the illnesses from which a small minority of them now get cured in hopsitals. There would be no poor-blooded and deformed children growing up in factories, no death rates, as now, of fifty per cent among children, no deterioration of whole generations, no prostitution, no syphilis, and no murdering of hundreds of thousands in wars, nor those horrors of folly and of misery which our present science considers a necessary condition of human life.

We have so perverted the conception of science that it seems strange to men of our day to allude to sciences which should prevent the mortality of children, prostitution, syphilis, the deterioration of whole generations, and the wholesale murder of men. It seems to us that science is only then real science when a man in a laboratory pours liquids from one jar into another, or analyzes the spectrum, or cuts up frogs and porpoises, or weaves in a specialized, scientific jargon an obscure network of conventional phrases—theological, philosophical, historical, juridical, or politico-economical—semi-intelligible to the man himself and intended to demonstrate that what now is, is what should be.

But science, true science—such science as would really deserve the respect which is now claimed by the followers of one (the least important) part of science—is not at all such as this: real science lies in knowing what we should and what we should not believe, in knowing how the associated life of man should and should not be constituted; how to treat sexual relations, how to educate children, how to use the land, how to cultivate it oneself without oppressing other people, how to treat foreigners, how to treat animals, and much more that is important for the life of man.

Such has true science ever been and such it should be. And such science is springing up in our times; but, on the one hand, such true science is denied and refuted by all those scientific people who defend the existing order of society, and, on the other hand, it is considered empty, unnecessary, unscientific science by those who are engrossed in experimental science.

For instance, books and sermons appear demonstrating the antiquatedness and absurdity of Church dogmas as well as the necessity of establishing a reasonable religious perception suitable to our times, and all the theology that is considered to be real science is only engaged in refuting these works and in exercising human intelligence again and again to find support and justification for superstitions long since outlived and which have now become quite meaningless. Or a sermon appears showing that land should not be an object of private possession, and that the institution of private property in land is a chief cause of the poverty of the masses. Apparently science, real science, should welcome such a sermon and draw further deductions from this position. But the science of our times does nothing of the kind: on the contrary, political economy demonstrates the opposite position—namely, that landed property, like every other form of property, must be more and more concentrated in the hands of a small number of owners. Again, in the same way, one would suppose it to be the business of real science to demonstrate the irrationality, unprofitableness, and immorality of war and of executions; or the inhumanity and harmfulness of prostitution; or the absurdity, harmfulness, and immorality of using narcotics or of eating animals; or the irrationality, harmfulness, and antiquatedness of patriotism. And such works exist, but are all considered unscientific, while works to prove that all these things ought to continue, and works intended to satisfy an idle thirst for knowledge lacking any relation to human life, are considered to be scientific.

The deviation of the science of our time from its true purpose is strikingly illustrated by those ideals which are put forward by some scientists and are not denied, but admitted, by the majority of scientific men.

These ideals are expressed not only in stupid, fashionable books, describing the world as it will be in 1000 or 3000 years' time, but also by sociologists who consider themselves serious men of science. These ideals are that food, instead of being obtained from the land by agriculture, will be prepared in laboratories by chemical means, and that human labor will be almost entirely superseded by the utilization of natural forces.

Man will not, as now, eat an egg laid by a hen he has kept, or bread grown on his field, or an apple from a tree he has reared and which has blossomed and matured in his sight, but he will eat tasty, nutritious food which will be prepared in laboratories by the conjoint labor of many people, in which he will take a small part. Man will hardly need to labor, so that all men will be able to yield to idleness as the upper, ruling classes now yield to it.

Nothing shows more plainly than these ideals to what a degree the science of our times has deviated from the true path.

The great majority of men in our times lacks good and sufficient food (as well as dwellings and clothes and all the first necessaries of life). And this great majority of men is compelled, to the injury of its well-being, to labor continually beyond its strength. Both these evils can easily be removed by abolishing mutual strife, luxury, and the unrighteous distribution of wealth—in a word, by the abolition of a false and harmful order and the establishment of a reasonable, human manner of life. But science considers the existing order of things to be as immutable as the movements of the planets and therefore assumes that the purpose of science is not to elucidate the falseness of this order and to arrange a new, reasonable way of life, but, under the existing order of things, to feed everybody and enable all to be as idle as the ruling classes, who live a depraved life, now are.

And meanwhile it is forgotten that nourishment with corn, vegetables, and fruit raised from the soil by one's own labor is the pleasantest, healthiest, easiest, and most natural nourishment, and that the work of using one's muscles is as necessary a condition of life as is the oxidation of the blood by breathing.

To invent means whereby people might, while continuing our false division of property and labor, be well nourished by means of chemically prepared food, and might make the forces of nature work for them, is like inventing means to pump oxygen into the lungs of a man kept in a closed chamber, the air of which is bad, when all that is needed is to cease to confine the man in the closed chamber.

In the vegetable and animal kingdoms a laboratory for the production of food has been arranged such as can be sur-

passed by no professors, and to enjoy the fruits of this laboratory and to participate in it, man has only to yield to that
ever joyful impulse to labor, without which man's life is a tor-
ment. And lo and behold! the scientists of our times, instead
of employing all their strength to abolish whatever hinders
man from utilizing the good things prepared for him, acknowledge the conditions under which man is deprived of
these blessings to be unalterable, and instead of arranging the
life of man so that he might work joyfully and be fed from
the soil, they devise methods which will cause him to become
an artificial abortion. It is like not helping a man out of confinement into the fresh air, but devising means, instead, to
pump into him the necessary quantity of oxygen and arranging so that he may live in a stifling cellar instead of living at
home.

Such false ideals could not exist if science were not on a
false path.

And yet the feelings transmitted by art grow up on the
bases supplied by science.

But what feelings can such misdirected science evoke? One
side of this science evokes antiquated feelings which humanity
has used up and which in our times are bad and exclusive.
The other side, occupied with the study of subjects unrelated
to the conduct of human life, by its very nature cannot serve
as a basis for art.

So art in our times, to be art, must either open up its own
road independently of science or must take direction from the
unrecognized science which is denounced by the orthodox section of science. And this is what art, when it even partially
fulfils its mission, is doing.

It is to be hoped that the work I have tried to perform concerning art will be performed also for science—that the falseness of the theory of science for science's sake will be demon-
strated; that the necessity of acknowledging Christian teaching in its true meaning will be clearly shown, that on the
basis of that teaching a reappraisement will be made of the
knowledge we possess and of which we are so proud; that the

secondariness and insignificance of experimental science, and the primary and importance of religious, moral, and social knowledge will be established; and that such knowledge will not, as now, be left to the guidance of the upper classes only, but will form a chief interest of all free, truth-loving men such as those who, not in agreement with the upper classes but in spite of them, have always forwarded the real science of life.

Astronomical, physical, chemical, and biological science, as also technical and medical science, will be studied only in so far as they can help to free mankind from religious, juridical, or social deceptions, or can serve to promote the well-being of all men and not of any single class.

Only then will science cease to be what it is now—on the one hand, a system of sophistries, needed for the maintenance of the existing worn-out order of society, and, on the other hand, a shapeles mass of miscellaneous knowledge, for the most part good for little or nothing—and become a shapely and organic whole having a definite and reasonable purpose comprehensible to all men, namely, the purpose of bringing to the consciousne of men the truths that flow from the religious perception of our times.

And only then will art, which is always dependent on science, be what it might and should be, an organ co-equally important with science for the life and progress of mankind.

Art is not a pleasure, a solace, or an amusement; art is a great matter. Art is an organ of human life, transmitting man's reasonable perception into feeling. In our age the common religious perception of men is the consciousness of the brotherhood of man—we know that the well-being of man lies in union with his fellow men. True science should indicate the various methods of applying this consciousness to life. Art should transform this perception into feeling.

The task of art is enormous. Through the influence of real art, aided by science guided by religion, that peaceful co-operation of man which is now obtained by external means—by our law courts, police, charitable institutions, factory inspection, etc.—should be obtained by man's free and joyous activity. Art should cause violence to be set aside.

And it is only art that can accomplish this.

All that now, independently of the fear of violence and punishment, makes the social life of man possible (and already now this is an enormous part of the order of our lives)—all this has been brought about by art. If people have been inculcated by art as to how they should treat religious objects, their parents, their children, their wives, their relations, strangers, foreigners; how to conduct themselves to their elders, their superiors, to those who suffer, to their enemies, and to animals; and if this has been obeyed through generations by millions of people, not only unenforced by any violence, but so that the force of such customs can be shaken in no way but by means of art— then, by the same art, other customs more in accord with the religious perception of our time may be evoked. If art has been able to convey the sentiment of reverence for images, for the eucharist, and for the king's person, of shame at betraying a comrade, devotion to a flag, the necessity of revenge for an insult, the need to sacrifice one's labor for the erection and adornment of churches, the duty of defending one's honor or the glory of one's native land—then that same art can also evoke reverence for the dignity of every man and for the life of every animal; can make men ashamed of luxury, of violence, of revenge, or of using for their pleasure that of which others are in need; can compel people freely, gladly, and without noticing it, to sacrifice themselves in the service of man.

The task for art to accomplish is to make that feeling of brotherhood and love of one's neighbor, now attained only by the best members of society, the customary feeling and the instinct of all men. By evoking under imaginary conditions the feeling of brotherhood and love, religious art will train men to experience those same feelings under similar circumstances in actual life; it will lay in the souls of men the rails along which the actions of those whom art thus educates will naturally pass. And universal art, by uniting the most different people in one common feeling, by destroying separation, will educate people to union, will show them, not by reason but by life itself, the joy of universal union reaching beyond the bounds set by life.

The destiny of art in our time is to transmit from the realm of reason to the realm of feeling the truth that well-being for men consists in being united together, and to set up in place of the existing reign of force that kingdom of God, i.e., of love, which we all recognize to be the highest aim of human life.

Possibly in the future science may reveal to art yet newer and higher ideals, which art may realize; but in our time, the destiny of art is clear and definite. The task for Christian art is to establish brotherly union among men.

APPENDICES

APPENDIX I [1]

This is the first page of Mallarmé's book, *Divagations:* [2]

Le Phénomène Futur

Un ciel pâle, sur le monde qui finit de décrépitude, va peut-être partir avec les nuages: les lambeaux de la pourpre usée des couchants déteignent dans une rivière dormant à l'horizon submergé de rayons et d'eau. Les arbres s'ennuient, et, sous leur feuillage blanchi (de la poussière du temps plutôt que celle des chemins) monte la maison en toile de Montreur de choses Passées: maint réverbère attend le crépuscule et ravive les visages d'une malheureuse foule, vaincue par la maladie immortelle et le péché des siècles, d'hommes près de leurs chétives complices enceintes des fruits misérables avec lesquels périra la terre. Dans le silence inquiet de tous les yeux suppliant là-bas le soleil qui, sous l'eau, s'enfonce avec le désespoir d'un cri, voici le simple boniment: "Nulle enseigne ne vous régale du spectacle intérieur, car il n'est pas maintenant un peintre capable d'en donner une ombre triste. J'apporte, vivante (et préservée à travers les ans par la science souveraine) une Femme d'autrefois. Quelque folie, originelle et naïve, une extase d'or, je ne sais quoi! par elle nommé sa chevelure, se ploie avec la grâce des étoffes autour d'un visage qu'éclaire la nudité sanglante de ses lèvres. A la place du vêtement vain, elle a un corps; et les yeux, semblables aux pierres rares! ne valent pas ce regard qui sort de sa chair heureuse: des seins levés comme

1 [Cf. Chapter X.—Ed.]

2 The translations in Appendices I and II are by Louise Maude. The aim of these renderings has been to keep as close to the originals as the obscurity of meaning allowed. The sense (or absence of sense) has therefore been more considered than the form of the verses.—Tr.

s'ils étaient pleins d'un lait éternel, la pointe vers le ciel, les jambes lisses qui gardent le sel de la mer première." Se rappelant leurs pauvres épouses, chauves, morbides et pleines d'horreur, les maris se pressent: elles aussi par curiosité, mélancoliques, veulent voir.

Quand tous auront contemplé la noble créature, vestige de quelque époque déjà maudite, les uns indifférents, car ils n'auront pas eu la force de comprendre, mais d'autres navrés et la paupière humide de larmes résignées, se regarderont; tandis que les poètes de ces temps, sentant se rallumer leur yeux éteints, s'achemineront vers leur lampe, le cerveau ivre un instant d'une gloire confuse, hantés du Rythme et dans l'oubli d'exister à une époque qui survit à la beauté.

The Future Phenomenon

A pale sky, above the world that is ending through decrepitude, going, perhaps, to pass away with the clouds: shreds of worn-out purple of the sunsets wash off their color in a river sleeping on the horizon, submerged with rays and water. The trees are weary and, beneath their foliage (whitened by the dust of time rather than that of the roads), rises the canvas house of "Showman of Things Past." Many a lamp awaits the gloaming, and brightens the faces of a miserable crowd vanquished by the immortal illness and the sin of ages, of men by the sides of their puny accomplices pregnant with the miserable fruit with which the world will perish. In the anxious silence of all the eyes supplicating the sun there, which sinks under the water with the desperation of a cry, this is the plain announcement: "No signboard now regales you with the spectacle that is inside, for there is no painter now capable of giving even a shadow of it. I bring living (and preserved by sovereign science through the years) a Woman of other days. Some kind of folly, naïve and original, an ecstasy of gold, I know not what! by her called her hair, clings with the grace of some material round a face brightened by the blood-red nudity of her lips. In place of vain clothing, she has a body; and her eyes, resembling precious stones! are not worth that look which comes from her happy flesh: breasts raised as if full of eternal milk, the points toward the sky; the smooth legs that keep the salt of the first sea." Remembering their poor spouses, bald, morbid, and full of horrors, the husbands press forward: the women, too, from curiosity, gloomily wish to see.

When all shall have contemplated the noble creature, vestige of some epoch already damned, some indifferently, for they will not have had strength to understand, but others, broken-hearted, and with eyelids wet with tears of resignation, will look at each other; while the poets of those times, feeling their dim eyes rekindled, will make their way toward their lamp, their brain for an instant drunk with confused glory, haunted by Rhythm and forgetful that they exist at an epoch which has survived beauty.

BAUDELAIRE'S FLOWERS OF EVIL

No. XXIV

I adore thee as much as the vaults of night,
O vase full of grief, taciturnity great,
And I love thee the more because of thy flight.
It seemeth, my night's beautifier, that you
Still heap up those leagues—yes! ironically heap!
That divide from my arms the immensity blue.

I advance to attack, I climb to assault,
Like a choir of young worms at a corpse in the vault;
Thy coldness, oh cruel, implacable beast!
Yet heightens thy beauty, on which my eyes feast!

No. XXXVI

DUELLUM

Two warriors come running, to fight they begin,
With gleaming and blood they bespatter the air;
These games, and this clatter of arms, is the din
Of youth that's a prey to the surgings of love.

The rapiers are broken! and so is our youth,
But the dagger's avenged, dear! and so is the sword,
By the nail that is steeled and the hardened tooth.
Oh, the fury of hearts aged and ulcered by love!

In the ditch, where the ounce and the pard have their lair,
Our heroes have rolled in an angry embrace;
Their skin blooms on brambles that erewhile were bare.

That ravine is a friend-inhabited hell!
Then let us roll in, oh woman inhuman,
To immortalize hatred that nothing can quell!

BAUDELAIRE'S LITTLE POEMS IN PROSE

THE STRANGER

Whom dost thou love best? say, enigmatical man—thy father, thy mother, thy brother, or thy sister?

"I have neither father, nor mother, nor sister, nor brother."

Thy friends?

"You there use an expression the meaning of which till now remains unknown to me."

Thy country?

"I ignore in what latitude it is situated."

Beauty?

"I would gladly love her, goddess and immortal."

Gold?

"I hate it as you hate God."

Then what do you love, extraordinary stranger?

"I love the clouds . . . the clouds that pass . . . there . . . the marvelous clouds!"

THE SOUP AND THE CLOUDS

My beloved little silly was giving me my dinner, and I was contemplating, through the open window of the diningroom, those moving architectures which God makes out of vapors, the marvelous constructions of the impalpable. And I said to myself, amid my contemplations, "All these phantasmagoria are almost as beautiful as the eyes of my beautiful beloved, the monstrous little silly with the green eyes."

Suddenly I felt the violent blow of a fist on my back, and I heard a harsh, charming voice, an hysterical voice, as it were hoarse with brandy, the voice of my dear little well-beloved, saying, "Are you going to eat your soup soon, you d—— b—— of a dealer in clouds?"

THE GALLANT MARKSMAN

As the carriage was passing through the forest, he ordered it to be stopped near a shooting gallery, saying that he wished to shoot off a few bullets to *kill* Time. To kill this monster, is it not the most ordinary and the most legitimate occupation of everyone? And he gallantly offered his arm to his dear, delicious, and execrable wife—that mysterious woman to whom he owed so much pleasure, so much pain, and perhaps also a large part of his genius.

Several bullets struck far from the intended mark—one even penetrated the ceiling; and as the charming creature laughed madly, mocking her husband's awkwardness, he turned abruptly toward her and said, "Look at the doll there on the right with the haughty mien and her nose in the air; well, dear angel, *I imagine to myself that it is you!*" And he closed his eyes and pulled the trigger. The doll was neatly decapitated.

Then, bowing toward his dear one, his delightful, execrable wife, his inevitable pitiless muse, and kissing her hand respectfully, he added, "Ah! my dear angel, how I thank you for my skill!"

VERLAINE'S FORGOTTEN AIRS

No. I

> "The wind in the plain
> Suspends its breath."—FAVART.

'Tis ecstasy languishing,
Amorous fatigue,
Of woods all the shudderings
Embraced by the breeze,
'Tis the choir of small voices
Toward the gray trees.

Oh, the frail and fresh murmuring!
The twitter and buzz,
The soft cry resembling
That's expired by the grass . . . .
Oh, the roll of the pebbles
'Neath waters that pass!

Oh, this soul that is groaning
In sleepy complaint!
In us is it moaning?
In me and in you?
Low anthem exhaling
While soft falls the dew.

No. VIII

In the unending
Dullness of this land,
Uncertain the snow
Is gleaming like sand.

No kind of brightness
In copper-hued sky,
The moon you might see
Now live and now die.

Gray float the oak trees—
Cloudlike they seem—
Of neighboring forests,
The mists in between

Wolves hungry and lean,
And famishing crow,
What happens to you
When acid winds blow?

In the unending
Dullness of this land,
Uncertain the snow
Is gleaming like sand.

SONG BY MAETERLINCK

When he went away,
(Then I heard the door)
When he went away,
On her lips a smile there lay . . .

Back he came to her,
(Then I heard the lamp)
Back he came to her,
Someone else was there . . .

It was death I met,
(And I heard her soul)
It was death I met,
For her he's waiting yet . . .

Someone came to say,
(Child, I am afraid)
Someone came to say
That he would go away . . .

With my lamp alight,
(Child, I am afraid)
With my lamp alight,
Approached I in affright . . .

To one door I came,
(Child, I am afraid)
To one door I came,
A shudder shook the flame . . .

At the second door,
(Child, I am afraid)
At the second door
Forth words of flame did pour . . .

To the third I came,
(Child, I am afraid)
To the third I came,
Then died the little flame . . .

Should he one day return
Then what shall we say?
Waiting, tell him, one
And for him dying lay . . .

If he asks for you,
Say what answer then?
Give him my gold ring
And answer not a thing . . .

Should he question me
Concerning the last hour?
Say I smiled for fear
That he should shed a tear . . .

Should he question more
Without knowing me?
Like a sister speak;
Suffering he may be . . .

Should he question why
Empty is the hall?
Show the gaping door,
The lamp alight no more . . .

APPENDIX II

No. 1

The following verses are by Vielé-Griffin, from page 28 of a volume of his poems:

Oiseau Bleu Couleur du Temps

1

Sait-tu l'oubli
D'un vain doux rêve,
Oiseau moqueur
De la forêt?
Le jour pâlit,
La nuit se lève,
Et dans mon coeur
L'ombre a pleuré;

2

O chante-moi
Ta folle gamme,
Car j'ai dormi
Ce jour durant;
Le lâche émoi
Où fut mon âme
Sanglote ennui
Le jour mourant . . . .

3

Sais-tu le chant
De sa parole
Et de sa voix,
Toi qui redis
Dans le couchant
Ton air frivole
Comme autrefois
Sous les midis?

4

O chante alors
La mélodie
De son amour,
Mon fol espoir,
Parmi les ors
Et l'incendie
Du vain doux jour
Qui meurt ce soir.

FRANCIS VIELÉ-GRIFFIN
Poèmes et Poésies

BLUE BIRD

1	2
Canst thou forget,	Thy tones let flow
In dreams so vain,	In maddening scale,
Oh, mocking bird	For I have slept
Of forest deep?	The livelong day;
The day doth set,	Emotions low
Night comes again,	In me now wail,
My heart has heard	My soul they've kept:
The shadows weep;	Light dies away . . . .

3	4
That music sweet,	Of my desire,
Ah, do you know	My hope so bold,
Her voice and speech?	Her love—up, sing,
Your airs so light	Sing, 'neath this light,
You who repeat	This flaming fire,
In sunset's glow,	And all the gold
As you sang, each,	The eve doth bring
At noonday's height.	Ere comes the night.

No. 2

And here are some verses by the esteemed young poet Verhaeren, which I also take from page 28 of his Works:

Attirances

Lointainement, et si étrangement pareils,
De grands masques d'argent que la brume recule,
Vaguent, au jour tombant, autour des vieux soleils.

Les doux lointaines!—et comme, au fond du crépuscle,
Ils nous fixent le coeur, immensément le coeur,
Avec les yeux défunts de leur visage d'âme.

C'est toujours du silence, à moins, dans la pâleur
Du soir, un jet de feu sondain, un cri de flamme,
Un départ de lumière inattendu vers Dieu.

On se laisse charmer et troubler de mystère,
Et l'on dirait des morts qui taisent un adieu
Trop mystique, pour être écouté par la terre!

Sont-ils le souvenir matériel et clair
Des éphèbes chrétiens couchés aux catacombes
Parmi les lys? Sont-ils leur regard et leur chair?

Ou seul, ce qui survit de merveilleux aux tombes
De ceux qui sont partis, vers leurs rêves, un soir,
Conquérir la folie à l'assaut des nuées?

Lointainement, combien nous les sentons vouloir
Un peu d'amour pour leurs oeuvres destituées,
Pour leur errance et leur tristesse aux horizons.

Toujours! aux horizons du coeur et des pensées,
Alors que les vieux soirs éclatent en blasons
Soudains, pour les gloires noires et angoissées.

ÉMILE VERHAEREN
Poèmes

ATTRACTIONS

Large masks of silver, by mists drawn away,
So strangely alike, yet so far apart,
Float round the old suns when faileth the day.

They transfix our heart, so immensely our heart,
Those distances mild, in the twilight deep,
Looking out of dead faces with their spirit eyes.

All around is now silence, except when there leap
In the pallor of evening, with fiery cries,
Some fountains of flame that Godward do fly.

Mysterious trouble and charms us infold,
You might think that the dead spoke a silent good-by,
Oh! too mystical far on earth to be told!

Are they the memories, material and bright,
Of the Christian youths that in catacombs sleep
'Mid the lilies? Are they their flesh or their sight?

Or the marvel alone that survives, in the deep,
Of those that, one night, returned to their dream
Of conquering folly by assaulting the skies?

For their destitute works—we feel it seems,
For a little love their longing cries
From horizons far—for their errings and pain.

In horizons ever of heart and thought,
While the evenings old in bright blaze wane
Suddenly, for black glories anguish fraught.

No. 3

And the following is a poem by Moréas, evidently an admirer of Greek beauty. It is from page 28 of a volume of his poems:

Énone au Clair Visage

Énone, j'avais cru qu'en aimant ta beauté
Où l'âme avec le corps trouvent leur unité,
J'allais, m'affermissant et le coeur et l'esprit,
Monter jusqu'à cela qui jamais ne périt,
N'ayant été crée, qui n'est froideur ou feu,
Qui n'est beau quelque part et laid en autre lieu;
Et me flattais encor' d'une belle harmonie
Que j'eusse composé du meilleur et du pire,
Ainsi que le chanteur qui chérit Polymnie,
En accordant le grave avec l'aigu, retire
Un son bien élevé sur les nerfs de sa lyre.
Mais mon courage, hélas! se pâmant comme mort,
M'enseigna que le trait qui m'avait fait amant

Ne fut pas de cet arc que courbe sans effort
La Vénus qui naquit du mâle seulement,
Mais que j'avais souffert cette Vénus dernière,
Qui a le coeur couard, né d'une faible mère.
Et pourtant, ce mauvais garçon, chasseur habile,
Qui charge son carquois de sagette subtile,
Qui secoue en riant sa torche, pour un jour,
Qui ne pose jamais que sur de tendres fleurs,
C'est sur un teint charmant qu'il essuie les pleurs,
Et c'est encore un Dieu, Énone, cet Amour.
Mais, laisse, les oiseaux du printemps sont partis,
Et je vois les rayons du soleil amortis.
Énone, ma douleur, harmonieux visage,
Superbe humilité, doux honnête langage,
Hier me remirant dans cet étang glacé
Qui au bout du jardin se couvre de feuillage,
Sur ma face je vis que les jours ont passé.

JEAN MORÉAS
Le Pèlerin Passionné

ENONE OF THE CLEAR VISAGE

Enone, in loving thy beauty, I thought,
Where the soul and the body to union are brought,
That mounting by steadying my heart and my mind,
In that which can't perish, myself I should find.
For it ne'er was created, is not ugly and fair;
Is not coldness in one part, while on fire it is there.
Yes, I flattered myself that a harmony fine
I'd succeed to compose of the worst and the best,
Like the bard who adores Polyhymnia divine,
And mingling sounds different from the nerves of his lyre,
From the grave and the smart draws melodies higher.
But, alas! my courage, so faint and nigh spent,
The dart that has struck me proves without fail
Not to be from that bow which is easily bent
By the Venus that's born alone of the male.

No, 'twas that other Venus that caused me to smart,
Born of frail mother with cowardly heart.
And yet that naughty lad, that little hunter bold,
Who laughs and shakes his flowery torch just for a day,
Who never rests but upon tender flowers and gay,
On sweetest skin who dries the tears his eyes that fill,
Yet oh, Enone mine, a God's that Cupid still.
Let it pass; for the birds of the Spring are away,
And dying I see the sun's lingering ray.
Enone, my sorrow, oh, harmonious face,
Humility grand, words of virtue and grace,
I looked yestere'en in the pond frozen fast,
Strewn with leaves at the end of the garden's fair space,
And I read in my face that those days are now past.

No. 4

And this is also from page 28 of a thick book, full of similar poems, by M. Montesquiou.

Berceuse d'ombre

Des formes, des formes, des formes
Blanche, bleue, et rose, et d'or
Descendront du haut des ormes
Sur l'enfant qui se rendort.
    Des formes!

Des plumes, des plumes, des plumes
Pour composer un doux nid.
Midi sonne: les enclumes
Cessent; la rumeur finit . . . .
    Des plumes!

Des roses, des roses, des roses
Pour embaumer son sommeil,
Vos pétales sont moroses
Près du sourire vermeil.
    O roses!

Des ailes, des ailes, des ailes
Pour bourdonner à son front,
Abeilles et demoiselles,
Des rythmes qui berceront.
    Des ailes!

Des branches, des branches, des branches
Pour tresser un pavillon,
Par où des clartés moins franches
Descendront sur l'oisillon.
    Des branches!

Des songes, des songes, des songes
Dans ses pensers entr'ouverts
Glissez un peu de mensonges
A voir la vie au travers.
    Des songes!

Des fées, des fées, des fées
Pour filer leurs écheveaux
Des mirages, de bouffées
Dans tous ces petits cerveaux.
    Des fées!

Des anges, des anges, des anges
Pour emporter dans l'éther
Les petits enfants étranges
Qui ne veulent pas rester . . . .
    Nos anges!

COMTE ROBERT DE MONTESQUIOU-FEZENSAC
Les Hortensias Bleus

THE SHADOW LULLABY

Oh forms, oh forms, oh forms
White, blue, and gold, and red
Descending from the elm trees,
On sleeping baby's head.
    Oh forms!

Oh feathers, feathers, feathers
To make a cozy nest.
Twelve striking: stops the clamor;
The anvils are at rest . . . .
      Oh feathers!

Oh roses, roses, roses
To scent his sleep awhile,
Pale are your fragrant petals
Beside his ruby smile.
      Oh roses!

Oh wings, oh wings, oh wings
Of bees and dragon-flies,
To hum around his forehead,
And lull him with your sighs.
      Oh wings!

Branches, branches, branches
A shady bower to twine,
Through which, oh daylight, faintly
Descend on birdie mine.
      Branches!

Oh dreams, oh dreams, oh dreams
Into his opening mind,
Let in a little falsehood
With sights of life behind.
      Dreams!

Oh fairies, fairies, fairies
To twine and twist their threads
With puffs of phantom visions
Into these little heads.
      Fairies!

Angels, angels, angels
To the ether far away,
Those children strange to carry
That here don't wish to stay . . . .
      Our angels!

APPENDIX III

These are contents of *The Nibelungen Ring:*

The first part tells that the nymphs, the daughters of the Rhine, for some reason guard gold in the Rhine, and sing: Weia, Waga, Woge du Welle, Walle zur Wiege, Wagala-weia, Wallala, Weiala, Weia, and so forth.

These singing nymphs are pursued by a dwarf (a nibelung) who desires to seize them. The dwarf cannot catch any of them. Then the nymphs guarding the gold tell the dwarf just what they ought to keep secret, namely, that whoever renounces love will be able to steal the gold they are guarding. The dwarf renounces love and steals the gold. This ends the first scene.

In the second scene a god and a goddess lie in a field in sight of a castle which giants have built for them. Presently they wake up and are pleased with the castle, and they relate that in payment for this work they must give the goddess Freia to the giants. The giants come for their pay. But the god Wotan objects to parting with Freia. The giants get angry. The gods hear that the dwarf has stolen the gold, promise to confiscate it, and to pay the giants with it. But the giants won't trust them, and seize the goddess Freia in pledge.

The third scene takes place underground. The dwarf Alberich, who stole the gold, for some reason beats a dwarf, Mime, and takes from him a helmet which has the power both of making people invisible and of turning them into other animals. The gods, Wotan and others, appear and quarrel with one another and with the dwarf and wish to take the gold, but Alberich won't give it up, and (like everybody all through the piece) behaves in a way to insure his own ruin. He puts on the helmet and becomes first a dragon and then a toad. The gods catch the toad, take the helmet off it, and carry Alberich away with them.

Scene IV. The gods bring Alberich to their home, and order him to command his dwarfs to bring them all the gold.

The dwarfs bring it. Alberich gives up the gold, but keeps a magic ring. The gods take the ring. So Alberich curses the ring and says it is to bring misfortune on anyone who has it. The giants appear; they bring the goddess Freia and demand her ransom. They stick up staves of Freia's height, and gold is poured in between these staves: this is to be the ransom. There is not enough gold, so the helmet is thrown in, and they also demand the ring. Wotan refuses to give it up, but the goddess Erda appears and commands him to do so because it brings misfortune. Wotan gives it up. Freia is released. The giants, having received the ring, fight, and one of them kills the other. This ends the Prelude, and we come to the First Day.

The scene shows a house in a tree. Siegmund runs in tired, and lies down. Sieglinda, the mistress of the house (and wife of Hunding), gives him a drugged draught, and they fall in love with each other. Sieglinda's husband comes home, learns that Siegmund belongs to a hostile race, and wishes to fight him next day; but Sieglinda drugs her husband and comes to Siegmund. Siegmund discovers that Sieglinda is his sister and that his father drove a sword into the tree so that no one can get it out. Siegmund pulls the sword out and commits incest with his sister.

Act II. Siegmund is to fight with Hunding. The gods discuss the question to whom they shall award the victory. Wotan, approving of Siegmund's incest with his sister, wishes to spare him, but, under pressure from his wife Fricka, he orders the Valkyrie Brünnhilda to kill Siegmund. Siegmund goes to fight; Sieglinda faints. Brünnhilda appears and wishes to slay Siegmund. Siegmund wishes to kill Sieglinda also, but Brünnhilda does not allow it, so he fights with Hunding. Brünnhilda defends Siegmund, but Wotan defends Hunding. Siegmund's sword breaks and he is killed. Sieglinda runs away.

Act III. The Valkyries (divine Amazons) are on the stage. The Valkyrie Brünnhilda arrives on horseback, bringing Siegmund's body. She is flying from Wotan, who is chasing her for her disobedience. Wotan catches her, and as a punishment dismisses her from her post as a Valkyrie. He casts a spell on her, so that she has to go to sleep and to continue asleep until a man wakes her. When someone wakes her she will fall in love with him. Wotan kisses her; she falls asleep. He lets off fire, which surrounds her.

We now come to the Second Day. The dwarf Mime forges a sword in a wood. Siegfried appears. He is a son born from the incest of brother with sister (Siegmund with Sieglinda), and has been brought up in this wood by the dwarf. In general, the motives of the actions of everybody in this production are quite unintelligible. Siegfried learns his own origin, and that the broken sword was his father's. He orders Mime to reforge it, and then goes off. Wotan comes in the guise of a wanderer and relates what will happen: that he who has not learned to fear will forge the sword and will defeat everybody. The dwarf conjectures that this is Siegfried and wants to poison him. Siegfried returns, forges his father's sword, and runs off, shouting, Heiho! heiho! heiho! Ho! ho! Aha! oho! aha! Heiaho! heiaho! heiaho! Ho! ho! Hahei! hoho! hahei!

And we get to Act II. Alberich sits guarding a giant, who, in the form of a dragon, guards the gold he has received. Wotan appears, and for some unknown reason foretells that Siegfried will come and kill the dragon. Alberich wakes the dragon and asks him for the ring, promising to defend him from Siegfried. The dragon won't give up the ring. Exit Alberich. Mime and Siegfried appear. Mime hopes the dragon will teach Siegfried to fear. But Siegfried does not fear. He drives Mime away and kills the dragon, after which he puts his finger, smeared with the dragon's blood, to his lips. This enables him to know men's secret thoughts, as well as the language of birds. The birds tell him where the treasure and the ring are, and also that Mime wishes to poison him. Mime returns, and says out loud that he wishes to poison Siegfried. This is meant to signify that Siegfried, having tasted dragon's blood, understands people's secret thoughts. Siegfried, having learned Mime's intentions, kills him. The birds tell Siegfried where Brünnhilda is and he goes to find her.

Act III. Wotan calls up Erda. Erda prophesies to Wotan and gives him advice. Siegfried appears, quarrels with Wotan, and they fight. Suddenly Siegfried's sword breaks Wotan's spear, which had been more powerful than anything else. Siegfried goes into the fire to Brünnhilda and kisses her; she wakes up, abandons her divinity, and throws herself into Siegfried's arms.

Third Day. Prelude. Three Norns plait a golden rope and talk about the future. They go away. Siegfried and Brünnhilda appear. Siegfried takes leave of her, gives her the ring, and goes away.

Act I. By the Rhine. A king wants to get married and also to give his sister in marriage. Hagen, the king's wicked brother, advises him to marry Brünnhilda and to give his sister to Siegfried. Siegfried appears; they give him a drugged draught which makes him forget all the past and fall in love with the king's sister, Gutrune. So he rides off with Gunther, the king, to get Brünnhilda to be the king's bride. The scene changes. Brünnhilda sits with the ring. A Valkyrie comes to her and tells her that Wotan's spear is broken, and advises her to give the ring to the Rhine nymphs. Siegfried comes, and by means of the magic helmet turns himself into Gunther, demands the ring from Brünnhilda, seizes it, and drags her off to sleep with him.

Act II. By the Rhine. Alberich and Hagen discuss how to get the ring. Siegfried comes, tells how he has obtained a bride for Gunther and spent the night with her, but put a sword between himself and her. Brünnhilda rides up, recognizes the ring on Siegfried's hand, and declares that it was he, and not Gunther, who was with her. Hagen stirs everybody up against Siegfried, and decides to kill him next day when hunting.

Act III. Again the nymphs in the Rhine relate what has happened. Siegfried, who has lost his way, appears. The nymphs ask him for the ring, but he won't give it up. Hunters appear. Siegfried tells the story of his life. Hagen then gives him a draught, which causes his memory to return to him. Siegfried relates how he aroused and obtained Brünnhilda, and everyone is astonished. Hagen stabs him in the back, and the scene is changed. Gutrune meets the corpse of Siegfried. Gunther and Hagen quarrel about the ring, and Hagen kills Gunther. Brünnhilda cries. Hagen wishes to take the ring from Siegfried's hand, but the hand of the corpse raises itself threateningly. Brünnhilda takes the ring from Siegfried's hand, and when Siegfried's corpse is carried to the pyre she gets onto a horse and leaps into the fire. The Rhine rises and the waves reach the pyre. In the river are three nymphs. Hagen throws himself into the fire to get the ring, but the nymphs seize him and carry him off. One of them holds the ring; and that is the end of the matter.

The impression obtainable from my recapitulation is, of course, incomplete. But however incomplete it may be, it is certainly infinitely more favorable than the impression which results from reading the four booklets in which the work is printed.